The Scottish Footballer

Bob Crampsey

BOB CRAMPSEY, a football fanatic and a collector of the game's memorabilia, is a contributor to the STV *Scotsport* programme. He has written the Centennial History of Queen's Park F.C.—a club of which he has been a life-long supporter—and, more recently, *World Cup Diary 1978*.

Since 1956 he has been a radio and television broadcaster, taking part in such programmes as *A Matter of Opinion*, *All Things Considered* and *What Do You Know?*—'Brain of Britain', which title he won in 1965.

Apart from his books on football, he has written studies of Puerto Rico and Guadeloupe, two plays—one of which was performed at the 1972 Edinburgh Festival—and numerous short stories. Three of his stories have appeared in successive issues of the Scottish Arts Council/Collins volume.

Married to a golfer who doctors occasionally, Bob Crampsey leads a busy working life as the Rector of St Ambrose High School, Coatbridge.

Cover illustration: Three 1930s' favourites: James Carabine (Third Lanark), William Mills (Aberdeen), Alec McSpadyen (Partick Thistle). (Cigarette cards by courtesy of W. D. & H. O. Wills.)

By the same author

THE GAME FOR THE GAME'S SAKE
(Centennial History of Q.P.F.C.)

PUERTO RICO

GUADELOUPE

WORLD CUP DIARY 1978

THE SCOTTISH FOOTBALLER

Bob Crampsey

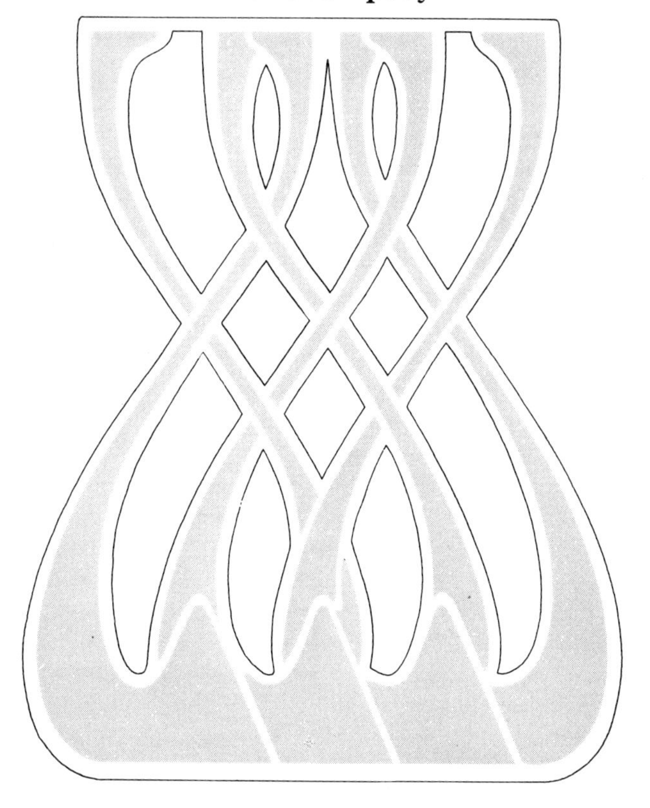

WILLIAM BLACKWOOD
1978

First published in 1978 by
William Blackwood & Sons Ltd
32 Thistle Street
Edinburgh EH2 1HA
Scotland

ISBN 0 85158 128 5

Printed at the Press of
the Publisher

Contents

Illustrations

Introduction

IN July 1971, in San Domingo, the capital of the Dominican Republic, I fell into conversation with an Italian naval officer from a cruiser which was paying a goodwill visit to the Caribbean. When, in answer to his inquiry, I told him I was from Scotland, he nodded amiably but non-committally. However, the additional information that I came from Glasgow brought an immediate roar of, "Jock Stein, Glasgow Celtic", and a delighted beckoning to his companions to sit in my reflected glory.

It is perhaps not surprising that in a country like Scotland, uncertain of its cultural identity, the professional footballer should be invested with the qualities of the folk-hero. When Celtic won the European Cup in 1967, they had done more than simply win a football competition. They had established Scottish pre-eminence in a field of activity regarded as important. A country which had produced no great playwright, musician, artist or poet (if we agree that Burns's major talent was that of a song-writer) was suddenly the champion of Europe at club level, and when in the following season Celtic lost narrowly to an Argentine side, they were still second best in the world.

Since Scotland has no parliament, no distinctive, widely spoken language, its most overt example of national feeling has been the annual soccer confrontation with England, unlovely as some of the manifestations of this nationalism have been. The Scottish footballer, frequently driven by circumstance to play in England for pay, has inherited the mantle of the Scottish mercenary soldier of the seventeenth and eighteenth centuries. He is the equivalent of the Spanish bullfighter, the French cyclist, the Russian ballerina, the American film star, and no one can really understand the life of industrial Scotland who does not appreciate the strength of football's appeal in the last hundred years, and the reasons for it.

A Scot, writing a poem such as Francis Thompson's 'At Lord's', with its beautiful and haunting ground-bass of 'O my Hornby and my Barlow long ago!', would not be short of evocative names—Bobby Templeton, R. S. McColl, Jimmy Quinn, Alan Morton, Jimmy McGrory, Tommy Walker, Gordon Smith, Denis Law—and still his omissions would annoy more readers than his inclusions would please.

For fully sixty years, in remuneration and life-style, the Scottish professional footballer filled the role of the aristocrat of the working-classes. He was not remote, as the music-hall stars were; he lived among the men whose admission money paid him, and he spoke and often dressed as they did. Football provided a chance, hazardous in the extreme, but at least a chance, of escaping the drudgery of nineteenth-century working-class life.

This passport to comparative temporary affluence had paradoxically been provided by an upper-class game. Association football, so soon to be claimed by the industrial masses as its very particular sport, had its origins in the ancient universities and great public schools of England. It was not of course envisaged there that this rough, turbulent game would ever provide a livelihood for anyone.

The game quickly made appeal to the Scottish worker. It was simple and pleasurable to watch or play. Unlike cricket, it was largely independent of weather, needed little equipment, and the playing pitch did not require the expensive cosseting of a cricket square.

The development of the game at amateur or professional level would not have been possible but for the shortening of the working-week and the availability for the first time of cheap and rapid transport to the general public. By 1880 increasing numbers of the working population were free of their employment by mid-Saturday afternoon at least, and the game was in the first instance a summer sport.

The railway boom had left central Scotland with an extensive system of transport, and whereas, off the railway lines, life moved at the pace of a horse, as it had done for centuries, connection between the major towns was by now speedy and certain.

If any one event could be said to have led to the eventual establishment of professional football in Scotland—a process which by the early 1970s resulted in such players as Billy McNeill of Celtic (see page 53) earning the equivalent of a senior Cabinet Minister's salary—it was the first international match between Scotland and England, fittingly played in Glasgow on St Andrew's Day, 1872.

The oldest Scottish football club, Queen's Park, founded five years earlier, were charged with making the arrangements for what was very much a trial venture. The public would watch football, but there was no guarantee that the public would pay to watch football, nor indeed was there a football ground available capable of holding a crowd of any size. West of Scotland Cricket Club were approached for the use of their ground at Hamilton Crescent, Partick. The rent agreed was ten pounds, with an additional ten pounds should the drawings exceed fifty pounds. In the event, about four thousand spectators paid almost one hundred and three pounds. The success of the match hastened the formation of the Scottish Football Association, making professionalism certain in the long run. The natural expertise of the Scots and their early successes against England soon led to their being in great demand by English clubs prepared to pay for their services.

One hundred years later, we have beaten England more times in international competition than she, a nation with ten times the resources, has beaten us. The Scottish footballer has given his country unlooked for and improbable success in these contests, and because of this he has been loved and venerated by the Scottish working-man.

Playing for Pay

IN a sense professionalism in Scotland was forced upon us by the English, for in the formative years of the game the Scots were infinitely superior. Of the first twelve internationals between the two countries, Scotland won eight and drew two. The clubs in the north of England wished to avail themselves of this rich vein of players, 'the Scotch professors' in the cant phrase of the day. Many Scots went south to Lancashire clubs such as Blackburn Rovers and Preston North End, and to the Birmingham area, where they turned out for Aston Villa and West Bromwich Albion. At first the professionalism was disguised; players would be offered money to play, but would also be found work at their own trades. In 1890, by which time professionalism in England had been legalised for more than five years, Blackburn Rovers offered Wilson, the goalkeeper of Vale of Leven, £3.10/- per week for playing and £1 a week for working at his own trade (as a dyer). Clearly the play was more important than the work.

Sometimes even this pretence was ignored. Notts County enticed J. Oswald, the international forward of Third Lanark, by offering him a tobacconist's shop stocked to the value of £500, and guaranteeing him two seven-month seasons, for each of which he was to receive £160. When we remember that in 1900 a fitter or a turner in Glasgow was receiving 36/- for a fifty-four-hour week, the attractions of football as a career became obvious. With jobs scarce in the country, then as now, Scotland would have been speedily drained of all her best players if she had remained amateur while players were being paid in England. More and more footballers took the train south, to become tobacconists or publicans or to spend the whole week unashamedly with 'no visible means of support', in the old police phrase. Full-time professionalism had come to stay south of the Tweed.

At first Scottish faces were rigorously set against following this example. It was pointed out that we had a much smaller population, a population, moreover, of which the great bulk was crammed into the Forth-Clyde Valley, and thus professionalism was not feasible. It would mean, as Queen's Park, the severest opponents of payment, pointed out, the speedy extinction from the top reaches of the game of country clubs such as Dumbarton, Vale of Leven and Renton.

This prophecy was to prove all too true, but it did little to halt the rising tide of opinion in favour of professionalism. A flourishing trade grew up in the poaching of Scots players by English 'agents'. This called forth the moral indignation of the Scottish sporting Press of the day. 'What Scot worthy of the name would be so base as to deliver a fellow-countryman into abject relations of total humiliation and subserviency?' thundered *Scottish Sport* in December 1888.

Of course the answer was that quite a few Scots would. These 'agents' led a harassed life; on at least two occasions at Ibrox and Kilmarnock they were physically chastised by supporters of Rangers and Kilmarnock, who had heard that southern spies were present on a tapping mission. The wretched Wilson, who went to Blackburn from Vale of Leven, was urged in the columns of *Scottish Sport* to 'Weigh against tempting gold the moral and physical shipwreck inseparable from the life of a professional football player'.

Officially there was a gap of eight years between the adoption of professionalism in England in 1885 and its acceptance in Scotland—but during those years under-the-counter payment had been rife. It was naïve to think that factory-hands and artisans, who supplied the great bulk of the players, could take two or three days from work to play friendly matches in England, which were very frequent, without being in some way compensated for loss of earnings and indemnified against the possible loss of jobs in an era of underemployment. With the exception of Queen's Park, who would have nothing to do with it, the payment of 'broken time', that is, compensation for wages lost at work, became common—and almost immediately was abused flagrantly.

In 1887 Hibernian won the Scottish Cup, defeating Dumbarton in the final. There were rumours of irregularities in the Hibs accounts, and the books were called in by the S.F.A. The Vale of Leven club, allies of Dumbarton, hired a private detective named Morton to do some investigating on the vanquished club's behalf. He discovered among other things that a Hibs player, Groves, an apprentice stonemason, whose wages were from 7/6d. to 10/- per week, was receiving 3/6d. for lost time on one morning alone, and that in a cup-tie week, when he was kept off work for three days, he had received £1 in broken time. Moreover, although Hibernian had had three secretary-treasurers in the previous five years, all the entries for that period were in the same hand. It was obviously a whitewash set of books, yet, astonishingly, Hibernian were cleared. Some weeks later, the Hibernian secretary, Mr McFadden, was reported as having absconded to Canada with club funds and money belonging to the Catholic diocese of Edinburgh!

The scandals grew in number and scope. Queen of the South Wanderers were convicted of making broken-time payments to two players, Lyle and Barbour, who were currently unemployed. The books of twenty-seven leading clubs were called in by the S.F.A. for scrutiny—Queen's Park, Rangers, Partick Thistle, Hearts and Hibs among them. The above-mentioned were cleared, but Cowlairs and St Bernard, two very powerful clubs in those days, were found guilty and suspended.

The advent of the late-coming but phenomenally successful Celtic club forced the issue, backed staunchly as they were by Rangers. Celtic could call upon the loyalties of the enormous Irish population in the West of Scotland, and with this captive audience their gates soon reached fantastic proportions. By 1890 they were drawing upwards of £5,000 per year. No club in Britain could equal that at this time. Even after improving the ground and contributing lavishly to charity, there was a good deal of money still floating. Many suspected that it floated to the players. In September 1889 the English *Athletic News* claimed that in the previous year the club had given £421 to charities, but their captain, James Kelly (father of Sir Robert Kelly, later President of the Scottish Football Association), had bought a public house at £650. 'Where had the money come from?'

Where indeed? There were several other prominent Glasgow players in like case. In defence of Celtic and Rangers it should be said that they were anxious that professionalism should be recognised openly, and the League gave them their chance. The A.G.M. of the S.F.A. in 1892 threw out a move for professionalism, but another try twelve months later was successful. By 1894 eighty-three clubs had registered almost 800 professional players.

Of course wages varied widely. Kilmarnock paid their lads 10/- per match and half a crown a point. Obviously money was not the main motive for pulling on a Kilmarnock shirt. Rich and poor soon sorted themselves out. In 1895 Celtic's weekly wage bill for players was £47, and Hearts' was £58, although the Tynecastle men included one or two expenses in theirs. Rangers paid more in wages to their second team in the same year than the Partick Thistle first team received. For the year ending May 1896, Rangers paid almost £2,000 in players' wages.

Professional football was established and continued unabated until the First World War. By that time, wages with run-of-the-mill First Division clubs such as Third Lanark and Hamilton Academicals had gone up to £3.10/- or £4 per week, roughly twice what a time-served tradesman could make. With the outbreak of war, full-time professional football was forbidden and the maximum wage reduced to £1 per game, although an additional £1 per game could be paid at the end of the season if gates warranted it.

The resumption of normal football in 1919 brought boom times—short-lived though they were—and the professional footballer was as well off as he was ever to be in the next thirty years. Provincial clubs such as Aberdeen and Dundee were paying their players £7 per week and the great Jimmy

McMullan of Partick Thistle was offered £9 per week with a £2 bonus for a win, £1 for a draw. Not happy with this offer, he demanded and got a transfer to Manchester City.

With the middle 1920s came slump. Even the great Patsy Gallagher was asked to take a cut in wages at Parkhead. He was very much at the veteran stage, but his pride was touched and he refused. He moved to Falkirk and spent five useful years with them to prove his point. Wages in the Second Division were rarely more than £2, and in the ill-fated Third Division, which lasted only two seasons, they verged on the ludicrous. Clubs such as Galston, Broxburn, Helensburgh and Brechin were paying as little as 10/- a match. No player could afford constantly to take time off work for this return—not with ten men chasing each job in industrial Scotland. The star player of the 1930s was indeed unlucky, bearing in mind the size of the crowds before which he performed. Frequently his audience was in excess of 100,000, but even the greatest players of the time, such as Bob McPhail of Rangers or Jimmy McGrory of Celtic, would rarely earn more than £8 a week.

Here are the testimonies of two of the great Scottish internationals of that time, Jerry Dawson of Rangers and Jimmy Delaney of Celtic (see illustrations on pages 9 and 10):

> "I signed for Rangers in season 1929-30. In my first season at Ibrox I was a part-timer, as I was completing my apprenticeship, so I played as a part-timer, training on Tuesday and Thursday nights. We were given to understand that there would be a very long apprenticeship to serve for our first-team places, about three to four years.
>
> "My parents were not at all keen on my playing professional football. They were less keen than ever when, in my first match against Celtic, the Celtic goalkeeper, John Thomson, sustained fatal injuries.
>
> "We were subject to very strict physical and social disciplines. Don't swim in fresh water, don't play badminton, be immaculate on the field, always run out of the tunnel, even if three down. To lose one's place in the side

and receive a free transfer was almost certainly to return to the Labour Exchange.

"We played in the palmy days of football. In the circumstances of the time we were millionaires. We paid income tax at the end of the year, and we made about £15 per week.* We had much better tours abroad than now. We went by boat, we had time to see the country, we lived like lords, and the opposition were pushovers. Now it is a very hasty flight and a really tough match."

(Interview with Jerry Dawson.)

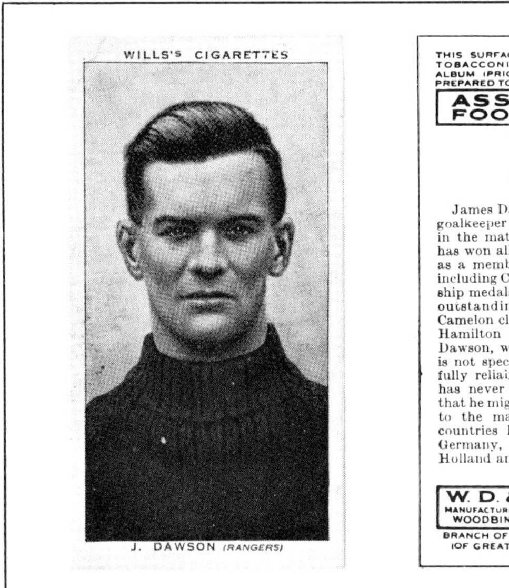

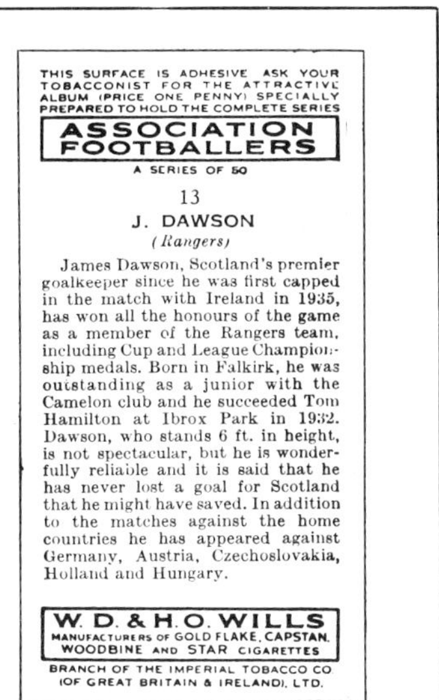

THIS SURFACE IS ADHESIVE ASK YOUR TOBACCONIST FOR THE ATTRACTIVE ALBUM (PRICE ONE PENNY) SPECIALLY PREPARED TO HOLD THE COMPLETE SERIES

ASSOCIATION FOOTBALLERS

A SERIES OF 50

13

J. DAWSON

(Rangers)

James Dawson, Scotland's premier goalkeeper since he was first capped in the match with Ireland in 1935, has won all the honours of the game as a member of the Rangers team, including Cup and League Championship medals. Born in Falkirk, he was outstanding as a junior with the Camelon club and he succeeded Tom Hamilton at Ibrox Park in 1932. Dawson, who stands 6 ft. in height, is not spectacular, but he is wonderfully reliable and it is said that he has never lost a goal for Scotland that he might have saved. In addition to the matches against the home countries he has appeared against Germany, Austria, Czechoslovakia, Holland and Hungary.

W. D. & H. O. WILLS

MANUFACTURERS OF GOLD FLAKE, CAPSTAN, WOODBINE AND STAR CIGARETTES

BRANCH OF THE IMPERIAL TOBACCO CO (OF GREAT BRITAIN & IRELAND), LTD.

"I signed for Celtic from Stoneyburn Juniors in 1934. As a provisional signing I was paid £2 per week. When I became a fully signed player, I got £4 per week, after which my wages went up by about 10/- per week each season. The most I ever got from Celtic was £7.10/-.

* At that time the Rangers club also paid bonuses to players on a twice-yearly basis.

During the war, of course, we were restricted to a maximum of £2 per match.

"When I moved to Manchester United in 1946, I stayed with them until 1950. The most I ever received at Old Trafford was £14-15. I then moved on to Aberdeen, to Falkirk, to Derry City, to Cork Celtic, and finally to Elgin City. I finished playing senior football in 1957.

"I had left school at fourteen and worked a short time in the pits, but I had been idle a good while when Celtic signed me. I lasted so long because I was a great trainer and was usually in bed by 10 p.m. I have arthritis now, caused by football, but I would do the same again. I would have liked to scout, not to manage. I would have loved to play in present-day football. When I was young I never thought the day would come when I would have to give up playing."

(Interview with Jimmy Delaney.)

THIS SURFACE IS ADHESIVE ASK YOUR TOBACCONIST FOR THE ATTRACTIVE ALBUM (PRICE ONE PENNY) SPECIALLY PREPARED TO HOLD THE COMPLETE SERIES

ASSOCIATION FOOTBALLERS

A SERIES OF 50

15

J. DELANEY

(Celtic)

A fast outside-right with a goal-scoring flair, James Delaney is a player with the big match temperament and he has been extremely successful in representative games. Born in Cleland, Lanarkshire, he learnt the game with the local club and joined Celtic in season 1933/34. He made his first appearance in the League team in the following season and after a short time made outside-right his own place. Delaney appeared against England in the King George V Jubilee Trust Fund Match in 1935, and he has since played against all the home countries as well as against Germany, Austria and Czechoslovakia.

W. D. & H. O. WILLS

MANUFACTURERS OF GOLD FLAKE, CAPSTAN, WOODBINE AND STAR CIGARETTES

BRANCH OF THE IMPERIAL TOBACCO CO (OF GREAT BRITAIN & IRELAND), LTD.

Despite this, the gifted footballer of the inter-war years was on balance much more fortunate than his industrial fellows, especially if he were able to work as well as play. There was no maximum wage in Scotland and one of the best ways for a player to make money from the game was to turn professional from Queen's Park. Any fee negotiated remained with the player and was paid as a weekly wage during his first professional season.

Alan Morton transferred from Queen's Park to Rangers in 1920 at a fee reputed to be £3,000, a most advantageous move. Interestingly, Morton was a mining engineer and had sufficient acumen to see the possibilities of such a shift. He dressed naturally in a city suit, tailored coat and bowler-hat, which earned him the sobriquet of 'The Wee Society Man'. The dress which he wore as a matter of course became compulsory garb for his Ibrox team-mates, on some of whom it sat less easily. William Struth, the Rangers' manager, was insistent on immaculate appearance on field and off. Morton was among the first professional footballers to become a director of one of the great British clubs.

The outbreak of war in 1939 again saw the imposition of a maximum wage, this time £2 per week, a crushing financial loss to those players who were engaged in top-class league football at the start of hostilities. The drastic reduction in wages was of course deliberately aimed at making full-time football impossible.

After 1945, the weekly wage packet slowly crept into double figures. For a time in the late 1940s and early '50s, Aberdeen, with £14 per week, led the Scottish pay scale. The club offered this high wage as a counter to geographical remoteness, for they insisted that all their players live in the town.

During the 1970s Celtic have been consistently the most successful club, so it is not strange that in paying their captain, Billy McNeill, about £15,000 per year they should establish a record for a Scottish footballer. The club manager, Jock Stein, when he reached the same mark, could reflect that he was being paid exactly a hundred times as much as the first Celtic manager, Willie Maley, who took office in the 1890s.

These wages are of course highly untypical, and in football, as in many other spheres, the rich get richer and the poor get poorer. In 1971 a Scottish club could retain the full-time services of a player for as little as £624 a year. More astonishing, a reasonable minimum wage for a Second Division player was set at £156, exactly twice what it was forty-seven years ago, whereas the price of food, transport and accommodation had multiplied several times. The explanation is that it was never imagined that playing for the majority of our Second Division clubs could ever be a full-time occupation. Nor is it, but what is anomalous is that the part-time and the full-time player sign exactly the same kind of contract.

Professional football is now, rightly, an accepted and an honourable occupation, astonishingly scandal free, when one considers the amount of money invested in it and wagered on it. It would be pleasant to think that as the players next Saturday move off in the special club bus, to arrive at a well-heated and well-equipped dressing-room, they could spare a thought for their forebears, jolting around the country in horse-brakes, or sitting up all night in smoke-filled carriages to England. As they sit under the treatment lamp let them think for a moment of the grimy men pushing their way off the cage as it reached the surface and running straight off to play; of the Motherwell player who, in the early days, collapsed after a cup-tie and on investigation was discovered to have worked a double-shift at a local blast-furnace in order to be available.

Let them remember too young Groves, the humble apprentice stonemason who, by accepting 3/6d., set the Scottish football world alight, over ninety years ago.

Social Status

OVER the past century, there has not been quite the widening of intake to professional football that might have been imagined. Football has always had its roots firmly set in industrial Scotland, rather than in the agricultural or commercial areas, and this remains true today.

It is not hard to find a noble lord connected with the game in the early days. The Earls of Rosebery have from the beginning had a connection with Hearts; Motherwell owed their ground to a gift from Lord Hamilton of Dalziel; and the Earl of Portland was a patron of Kilmarnock. Lord Rosebery and the Marquis of Lorne were Honorary Presidents of the S.F.A. These gentlemen were names on a letterhead rather than active legislators, however, and the game drew its strength from mine, factory and foundry.

Initially there was a fierce prejudice against the paid player. 'Base mercenary', 'Hired man-at-arms' and, in the case of those who dared to go to England, 'Traitorous wretches', were some of the kindest descriptions the Press of the 1890s had for them. It was an age of more open social prejudice and class distinction than our own; nevertheless the severity with which poor and unemployed young men were condemned for taking the Saxon shilling is startling and unpleasant.

It was assumed that every Scot who crossed the Tweed would end up as the drunken proprietor of a disreputable pub—'dram shop' was the term used. Great was the horror when Quentin Neil and Harry Miller of Queen's Park fell to the temptation of English gold. In the words of *Scottish Sport*, 'Now a higher social scale is touched.' Queen's Park certainly had a larger proportion of students, apprentice accountants and commercial travellers than most clubs. They were regarded as a snobbish lot, and it was widely believed, long after it had been proved false, that Hampden players would not sit down at the same table with professionals. When a full-back, Ritchie of Renton, expressed a wish to play for Queen's Park, the papers were quick to let it be known that 'He comes of good family'.

Footballers did not, of course, always get a bad press. By the mid-1890s the Glasgow Charity Cup could raise the astonishing sum of £1,800 in a year for local institutions. Soon clergymen, particularly ministers of the Church of Scotland and Catholic priests, were giving the game and its players encouragement and support. Not so the Free Church, in whose General Assembly the Reverend John McNeill denounced the new pastime as 'A wile of the serpent'. He claimed that people were so busy discussing the previous day's game that they stayed away from church, with a disastrous effect on collections.

In general, though, references to footballers and football continued to be patronising. When a competition was established for Glasgow warehouse firms, it was noted that 'This can work only good for the pale, languid members of the artisan class'. Much the same thing was said by Mr Lewis McIver, Unionist candidate for an Edinburgh constituency, who declared, 'It [football] is an educative pastime—it makes hardy youths of clerks and shopmen who without it might be weaklings. Better is it for our youth to be in the open air than in the tavern.'

In the tavern some of the players undoubtedly were. There was a famous Celtic-Dumbarton match at New Year time, when Celtic conceded eight goals, and not all their players were pillars of sobriety, or so it was widely rumoured. Football was not yet the deadly serious business it was to become. At Parkhead in an early Scottish cup-tie against a country side, the Celtic goalkeeper, anticipating that there would not be much coming his way, kept his ordinary trousers on. In the famous 'Snow Final' between Third Lanark and Celtic, both sides snowballed the crowd, while at the same time singing 'Two Lovely Black Eyes'. This impromptu entertainment drew heavy criticism from the Press as being both undignified and irresponsible.

It says much for the stamina and good humour of the players that they had the inclination for such romps; the life of the early professional was hard. When Dumbarton played Hearts in the Scottish Cup Final of 1891, the Dumbarton players worked as usual until breakfast-time, then met and dined together before catching the train. Striking workers, knowing that they would get a sympathetic response from the industrial crowds flocking to matches, were in the habit of taking up collections at football grounds. In 1892 the Bridgeton weavers collected £25 at Celtic Park and £9 at other grounds.

Gradually the game acquired a certain amount of social tone. In 1893 Her Royal Highness the Princess Mary, later Queen Mary, attended the England-Scotland match at Richmond. In 1895, when the secretaryship of the Football Association became vacant, barristers, solicitors and schoolmasters were among the applicants for the post. Footballers, it was realised, could now mix in polite society. Five years after Dumbarton players had put in a morning's work in Denny's Shipyard on Cup Final Day, Hearts spent the week before the big match in an Edinburgh hotel; to while away the time they went to theatres, to the circus and played golf near Gullane. These excursions were partly owing to beneficent paternalism and partly to an early attempt to remove players from the energy-sapping attentions of their wives.

The game in Scotland was beginning to be concerned with its image. The S.F.A. was not delighted when a sporting paper began to run a rudimentary form of football pool offering a prize of ten pounds, the winner being the person who guessed four scores correctly.

The competition survived S.F.A. disapproval, for the prize-money was large by turn-of-the-century standards, but the manufacturers of Bovril were less successful when they offered to present eleven gold medals to the Scottish Cup winners in return for the advertising. The offer was spurned indignantly. There was no truck with commercial sponsorship until the 1960s, but then the game in Scotland began to take money from the pools firms and from such tournaments as the Drybrough and Texaco Cups, in which the sponsors provided prize-money and underwrote the expenses of the competition. In 1977 the final citadel was breached when the historic Scottish Cup itself was given over to sponsorship.

Until 1914 it would in general be true to say that any lawyer, doctor or teacher playing football in Scotland would be wearing a Queen's Park jersey. There were exceptions, but the rule held good. After the Armistice, things began to change, although the change was slow, and the stigma attached to a professional man playing professional football had not entirely vanished even by 1939. The change occurred for two main reasons. First, the more astute schoolboys saw that professional football could finance their academic studies. Second, it became increasingly more awkward for a player to play as an amateur with a professional club. An amateur's presence was a potential cause of trouble among the players, a risk many managers refused to contemplate.

By the 1930s Rangers regulars included Dr Marshall, George Brown, their present director, who was a schoolteacher, and T. H. Soutar, a lawyer who was signed from Queen's Park, although his career at Ibrox was brief. In Edinburgh Tommy Walker, Tynecastle's darling first as player and later as manager (see page 17), had originally intended to be a minister, a career frustrated by the war. Matt Lynch of Celtic was a graduate and it looked as though this might well be the future pattern of the game.

Even after the prolonged interruption caused by Hitler, it seemed as if professional football would no longer be the exclusive preserve of the traditional working-class lad. In the years immediately following 1945, Aberdeen had Tony Harris, a dentist; Hibernian had John Cuthbertson, with the Ministry of Labour; Rangers had John Little, Bobby Brown and Derek Grierson, all teachers. The Celtic content of graduates was always very small, partly because they did not make a practice of taking Queen's Park players.

SURFACE IS ADHESIVE ASK YOUR TOBACCONIST FOR THE ATTRACTIVE ALBUM (PRICE ONE PENNY) SPECIALLY PREPARED TO HOLD THE COMPLETE SERIES

ASSOCIATION FOOTBALLERS

A SERIES OF 50

45

T. WALKER

(Heart of Midlothian)

A player who seized the imagination of the Scottish football public almost at once on his appearance in the Heart of Midlothian team, Tommy Walker has fully retained his popularity. Born in the village of Livingston Station, Midlothian, Walker played with Broxburn Rangers and Linlithgow Rose before joining Hearts at the age of seventeen in season 1932/33. Previously he had won international honours as a schoolboy and he has now eighteen senior caps to his credit, including those for matches against Germany, Czechoslovakia, Holland and Hungary as well as those against the home countries.

W. D. & H. O. WILLS

MANUFACTURERS OF GOLD FLAKE, CAPSTAN, WOODBINE AND STAR CIGARETTES

BRANCH OF THE IMPERIAL TOBACCO CO. (OF GREAT BRITAIN & IRELAND), LTD.

The number of graduates in Scottish football has not, however, significantly increased over the last twenty years. Two events have conspired to limit the numbers. One has little to do with football itself. It is simply that since the 1920s a number of good academic schools which used to play football have gone over to rugby, wholly or in part, and this has diminished the flow of potential players from middle-class and academic backgrounds.

The other reason is the change in the game itself, with the tremendous increase in the scope of European competition. At top level in the game today, it is virtually impossible to be a first-team man and do justice to one's profession. No doctor can ask a patient to wait for two or three days till he returns from Budapest, nor would a lawyer be popular who held up a house purchase while he played in Hamburg. Recent exceptions, such as Jim Craig of Celtic and Donald Ford of Hearts, will be found to have co-operative partners. The future of the graduate in professional football lies, in my view, somewhere below very top level. The big clubs want all their players' time and they want it from a very early age. John McHugh of Clyde and Dennis McQuade of Partick Thistle could combine academic work and football because neither of their clubs had European commitments. Ironically, it is the less successful teams in Scottish football who seem destined to have the broadest-based range of players' occupations, while Rangers, Celtic and their immediate challengers continue to recruit in those areas where they have always done. This, after all, is what full-time football entails. The academic boy may have to settle for something less than the top rewards on the field.

Trains, Trams and Tearaways

W. S. GILBERT had some harsh things to say about 'The idiot who praises, with enthusiastic tone, all centuries but this, and every country but his own'. We are apt to deplore the conduct of crowds at football matches these days, and to imagine that there has been a sharp and recent deterioration in the conduct of the spectators. A glance at old newspapers and documents is enough to prove otherwise. Witness a newspaper report of a Scottish cup-tie between Queen's Park and Vale of Leven in 1876. 'Yelling, hooting and calling out the players by cognomens [nicknames] were nothing to the coarse and vulgar pleasantries indulged in. Happily, there were no ladies present in the vitiated atmosphere.'

In a more formal sphere, a directive of the Referee's Committee of the S.F.A. in 1909 deplored the increase in the use of obscene language, ratchets, whistles and other annoyances. These distressing habits by no means kept all women away from football matches. There were large numbers of ladies in attendance in the early days, and in that more gallant age they were admitted free of charge and continued to be until the close of the First World War. In 1892 one damsel caused a sensation when she appeared in the stand at Ibrox Park smoking a big cigar. There was a travelling ladies' football team under the management of Lady Florence Dixie, which played exhibition matches at Love Street and Cappielow among other places, but the newspapers of the day were both jeering and censorious. A sample comment was, 'One of the full-backs was suspected of playing in her brother's knickers. The fair player was frequently asked for the name of her tailor.'

At the end of the nineteenth century, the crowds watching football were the greatest ever to assemble on a peaceful occasion, and in a harder, more violent age, it is not surprising that occasionally there should have been disorder.

The possibility of trouble was heightened by the fact that several of the Scottish clubs had strong Irish connections in an age when Home Rule for Ireland was the great political question of the day. The club most strongly associated with the Home Rule movement was Hibernian, so much so that when they played in London for the first time and the players were given a free day, they went to the Law Courts to see the trial of one Pigott, who had forged letters purporting to involve the Irish leader, Charles Stewart Parnell, in the Phoenix Park murders.

Disorder in Scottish football and its spilling over into social life is most commonly associated with the rivalry between Celtic and Rangers. From the beginning their relationship was an odd one. In the early stages the two clubs were particularly friendly. They travelled by the same railway coach on New Year trips to England. The first Scottish League Secretary, Mr J. H. McLaughlin of Celtic, was for several years accompanist to the Rangers Glee Club and Choir. Players moved between Parkhead and Ibrox quite freely. Matches between the two clubs were played in perfect amity. There was a famous occasion in 1892 when, although 19,000 people attended an Old Firm (then a very young firm) fixture at Ibrox, there was not one arrest, and for the first time in memory no Govan Police Court on the Monday morning.

Things did not always go so smoothly, although trouble on the terraces was usually kindled by events on the field. In one of the most inaccurate prophecies of all time, *Scottish Sport* announced in August 1896, 'Nothing will sooner cool the public interest in the meetings of Celtic and Rangers than frequent displays of bad blood.' Celtic were regarded as an Irish club, although from the beginning they signed Scottish Protestants; they were frequently referred to in the sporting Press as 'The Irishmen', and the selection of two of their players for a Scottish international side was the signal for a shoal of letters to the papers furiously inquiring whether eleven 'genuine' Scotsmen could not be found, a point of view which *Scottish Sport* slapped down hard.

Not all the bother arose from this airt. Often it was merely the exuberance of local supporters. One referee declared nervously after handling a Scottish cup-tie between Queen's Park and Broxburn Shamrock at the latter's ground, "Had it not been for the presence of the police, I would have been manhandled had the Shamrock lost."

There were some who did not share this referee's high opinion of the police. The original Cathkin Park, home of Third Lanark Football Club, was bisected by the Renfrewshire-Lanarkshire boundary, and in an early match at which fighting broke out, the Renfrewshire police were severely castigated because they simply shepherded the brawlers over the county line into Lanarkshire, and then stood back and admired proceedings. The charge for the services of a policeman was four shillings a day, and eight constables were the normal complement at a Second Division game. From time to time the police authorities were blamed for disregarding the wishes of the clubs in respect of the number of police they considered necessary to maintain order. There was trouble at Parkhead in a match against Rangers in 1896, resulting in complaints about poor police supervision. 'The effete handful of constables at Parkhead on Saturday was a disgrace to the Second City of the Kingdom.'

Sometimes the trouble was due to a failure to keep the crowd informed of developments. This was the cause of the Hampden Riot of 1909; and in more recent times, in 1952, the crowd at Cathkin stopped a friendly being played between Third Lanark and Celtic after the pitch had been declared unfit for a cup-tie.

In one respect the rowdies of the nineteenth century lagged behind our current crop. Railways made competitive football possible, but there is little or no evidence of damage to rolling-stock by depressed or infuriated supporters. In 1888 the first special train had been run from Birmingham to Glasgow in connection with an F.A. cup-tie between Queen's Park and Aston Villa, played oddly enough at Titwood (better known in Scottish sport as the home of

Clydesdale Cricket Club). Not that this excursion was without incident. Queen's thrashed Villa 6-1, and many Brummies missed the train back for—but let the contemporary account speak for itself: 'They were driven to refresh themselves by the wine of the country, and indulged in such excessive potations that they lay in the streets where they fell, like the members of a conquered army.' Before 1914 railway companies would send a pilot engine ahead to Dundee to keep the lines clear for football specials from Glasgow. The tramways put on special services for Glasgow and Edinburgh big matches, and the new Glasgow Underground derived much of its revenue from the happy fact that Copeland Road station was adjacent to Ibrox.

Brawling, however, was bad for the game, and particularly for the future of the sport. With virtually every riot, every bad incident, another school would desert soccer for rugby. Competitive football was played at school level in Scotland from an early date. The famous and venerable Airdrie Schools Tournament attracted large crowds; and more than 12,000 people watched the final of the Inspectors' Cup in Edinburgh before the turn of the century. Yet in many quarters it was thought not to be a respectable pastime. The old gibe, 'A gentleman's game played by hooligans', made its appearance. It came to be generally accepted that the 'better' schools played rugby, and the less socially select contented themselves with soccer. The Merchant Company schools in Edinburgh, the more famous Corporation schools of that city, the boarding schools, all played rugby. In the years since the First World War, three of Glasgow's most famous schools, Hutcheson's Grammar, Allan Glen's and St Aloysius's College, have forsaken football for the more vigorous but less skilful game of rugby.

There has been much talk of the innate virtues of rugby, the teaching of courage, and the willingness of players to accept the referee's decision, but the last-named virtue is largely influenced by the fact that rugby is an amateur game and a bad decision is irritating but not financially painful. The manliness complex suppresses other reasons, such as the

Willie Woodburn (Rangers)

Lawrie Reilly (Hibernian)

utilitarian advantage of being able to give thirty boys a game in the same space used by twenty-two, and the opportunity in rugby for the big, clumsy boy, who would flounder on a soccer field.

A boy attending a rugby school is not necessarily lost to soccer. In time past Willie Woodburn of Rangers and Lawrie Reilly of Hibs (see page 23) attended schools where rugby predominated, and of today's players, Harry Hood of Celtic and Bobby Clark of Aberdeen did likewise. From whatever scholastic background, the fact remains that on this coming Saturday, a staggering total of more than 50,000 Scots will be playing football. It is still, as it was described long ago, 'A game rooted in the people'.

The Early Greats

IN the first years of the twentieth century Scottish professional football began to be affected by the cult of personality. Such players as Nick Smith of Rangers, Jimmy Quinn of Celtic, Jimmy Brownlie of Third Lanark, Bobby Templeton of Kilmarnock (see page 31) were all household names. Their weekly fortunes were followed avidly in the newspapers which had begun to devote considerable space to their activities. In September 1884 the Glasgow *Evening News* produced the first-ever football edition of a newspaper, giving scores in matches played that afternoon. In addition, publications such as *Scottish Referee, Scottish Umpire* and *Scottish Sport* provided an eager readership with comment on games and anecdotes about the game's personalities.

Before 1914 it was unusual for a professional man to play professional football, and indeed even in the inter-war period such an occurrence was not common. Prominent footballers almost always came from an industrial background, but R. S. McColl was an exception. As a clerk, he had played for the amateur Queen's Park and had scored a hat-trick against England in the Rosebery International of 1900, when the Scottish team appeared in the racing colours of that nobleman. McColl subsequently turned professional with Rangers and later moved to Newcastle United.

In an unprecedented and unrepeated occurrence, he was reinstated as an amateur with Queen's Park, a contentious move which shook the venerable club to its foundations. On his retirement from playing, he built up a chain of confectionery shops which became renowned throughout Scotland and beyond. As early as 1910 the 'inevitable dram-shop' tag was being removed from the ex-professional. 'Toffee Bob', as McColl was known, has some claim to be the first entrepreneur among Scottish footballers.

There had been a logical progression from the unpaid

player to the professional player to the full-time footballer. By the first decade of the twentieth century, the city clubs in Glasgow and Edinburgh were regularly attracting crowds of 20,000 and upwards. They naturally wished control of the disposition of their players, and since they paid well—the average wage for a Rangers, Celtic or Hearts player at that time was £4 per week—the players were perfectly happy to go full-time. In any event, the life of a miner such as Quinn, or a bricklayer such as Brownlie, was too arduous to combine with top-level professional football.

James Quinn was a Homeric figure. He came from the Dunbartonshire village of Croy, and had the powerful shoulders and trunk of the miner. Of middle height, he was renowned for the vigour of his charging but was universally admitted to be a scrupulously fair opponent. He was one of the very earliest Scottish players to lend his name to advertising. In a football handbook of 1913 he is to be found testifying to the efficacy of Boag's Rheumatic Rum (see page 27). The rum, which retailed at the rather up-market price of one shilling per bottle, was also a sovereign specific in cases of neuralgia, toothache, lumbago and tic douloureux, from all of which the redoubtable James had apparently suffered in his time.

The players at the top were doing very well in financial terms. The great Scottish winger, Bobby Templeton of Kilmarnock, noted for his immaculate on-field appearance and excessively neat centre-shed hair parting, was sufficient of an attraction to be paid throughout the twelve-week close season, always an important indication of status. From the wage book of Kilmarnock Football Club for 1911-12 we get a good idea of his earnings. He was paid £4 per week the year round and a bonus of 5/- for every league point gained. His income from league matches alone was therefore £216 in that season, and to that sum must be added an allowance for cup-ties and international appearances. Also, since alone among his team-mates his address was given as the Royal Hotel, Kilmarnock, it is possible that his accommodation was subsidised to some extent, and that his total earnings could be set

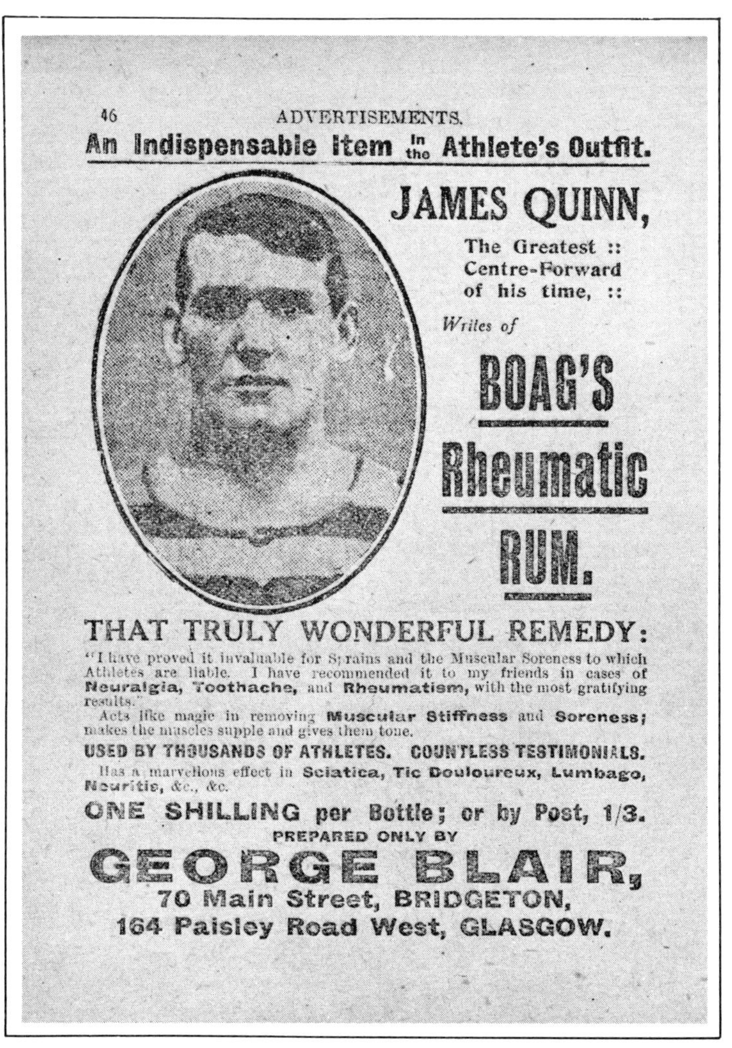

A glowing testimonial. One of the earliest examples of footballing sponsorship

in the region of £240 per annum. To earn this sum was to be comfortably off, for at that time a carpenter commanded 42/6d. for a 52½ hour week, and a shoemaker a mere 30/-. In

1914 a good First Division footballer was approximately twice as well paid as a worker in a skilled trade. This was a pattern which would hold good for another half-century.

Much more convincing than a recital of wages paid is the robust voice of Jimmy Brownlie, Third Lanark and Scotland goalkeeper. In his ninetieth year, in 1973, he looked back across the century to his days as a young professional footballer:

> "My first game I saved two penalty kicks against Partick Thistle and we won 2-1. It was a mid-week game and I thought that was a good start for me. Well, as it turned out, it *was* a good start and it gave me that confidence to go on. Seventeen years with them after that and they were very good to me and while I was getting caps they were always giving me rises in my wages and my pay came up to about £11 with international caps. But that was how the pay went up. In the summer holidays came the close season—they gave me £30 to go down to the coast for a holiday, just a fortnight, which I thought was very nice outside the rise in my wages."

Brownlie was very charitable towards the modern player, but he evinced a certain pride in the Spartan conditions of his own youth:

> "The facilities when I was playing were nothing like what they are today but they were very good as far as we were concerned. The old trainer gave me a hot-water bath and a sponge. That was all they had, and my training was three or four laps round the ground and then fourteen sprints, maybe less, and then the punch-ball behind the stand. High balls behind the stand to practise catching them, then the punch-ball, both punch-balls, and then the skipping-ropes, a hot bath and plunge into the cold bath, come out and the trainer rubbed you down and gave you a rub with the old-fashioned gloves they had in those days, with their hand, you know, no massaging, although massaging did come a wee bit later in my career, but there

wasn't so much massaging in my time, it was all rubbing with your hand. I never had many sores or bruises, the only sore I had was my pinkie."

The old man had been one of the greatest Scotland goalkeepers of all time, but until his death he retained a sense of genuine wonder at his elevation, and this awe-struck impression comes over clearly as he talks about his contemporaries:

"We were all treated well, and I'll tell you this, there was a competition in the *Weekly Record* then, you can advertise that because it's not the *Weekly Record* now, there was a competition for the three most popular players in Scotland— Jimmy Quinn, Alex Smith and myself got three cups from the general public. I've got the cup in the house yet, and a nice wee cup it is and I thought it was a great honour to me to be competing against these, Alex Smith and Jimmy Quinn, because they were longer in the game than me and I thought it was a great honour on myself."

By 1921 Brownlie was just as famous as the men he idolised. He was in the first group of Scottish players to tour Canada, and he manages to convey both the heavy schedule of fixtures and the leisurely mode of transportation of that tour:

"I remember we went on tour in 1921 and we travelled by boat from Liverpool to Halifax. We travelled to Halifax, from Halifax to Montreal, Montreal on to Ottawa, Ottawa on to Hamilton, Hamilton back to Ottawa, Ottawa back to Regina, Saskatchewan, on to Toronto, Toronto to Winnipeg, Winnipeg to Edmonton, Edmonton to Calgary, Calgary to Vancouver. The dollars worked out about £28.10/- per man, so that was very good. We landed in Montreal and played the championship with Canada and before I finish wait till I tell a story. The best white black man ever I met was the attendant in the car—he was racing for Halifax right through the whole of Canada and back, and if you lost a button off your shirt or lost anything, he was going about looking for it. At the station he was standing with his wife and family, I think there was about a dozen of a family, I'm not right sure, but there was a crowd anyway. There were tears running down his eyes thanking us and we gave him £25, that's what he got between the Association and the players."

The older players who toured in the days of ships and trains are vehement in their belief that they took part in the last of the enjoyable tours. 'The difference between a sailor's shore leave from a cargo ship and the modern fellow's lightning turn-round on a tanker', was how it was described to me. Certainly players on tour, even within the British Isles, lived well, stayed in expensive hotels, and even before 1900 were travelling to away matches by train in private saloon coaches. The coming of professionalism did not immediately cut all traces of amateur attitudes. It remained for some years a tradition for clubs to give their players expensive wedding presents.

Not all players were Brownlies, Smiths or Quinns. There had been a time between the inception of professionalism and the formation of football clubs into limited-liability companies when the footballer who had a grievance, real or imagined, about wages, was at a severe disadvantage. Any action he might raise would lie against the membership individually, and since most players lacked the knowledge or resources to pursue such an action, many were bilked. Despite this hazard, by the end of the Edwardian era it was clearly a paying proposition to play top-class professional football in Scotland.

Jimmy Brownlie (Third Lanark)

Bobby Templeton (Kilmarnock)

The Scots Player in England Since 1918

DR JOHNSON's dictum that 'the noblest prospect which a Scotchman ever sees, is the high road that leads him to England' certainly holds true for the footballer of the northern kingdom. From the resumption of normal football in 1919 until the present time, the roads and railways have transported south a ceaseless cargo of our most skilled players.

Simple economics and population distribution have made this inevitable. Of the Scottish clubs, only Celtic and Rangers could consistently match English wages. It is true that there was no maximum wage in Scotland, but obviously the going rate bore an extremely close relation to the maximum wage pertaining in England, which fluctuated between £6 and £8 per week in the inter-war years.

Occasionally other Scottish clubs, such as Motherwell in the 1930s and Hibernian in the early 1950s, managed to keep star-studded sides together for comparatively brief periods. More usually, any Scottish player was made available for transfer if the price offered was sufficiently tempting. Great exponents of the Scottish game, such as Alec James and John White, played the bulk of their league football in England. Even more galling from the home enthusiast's view was the fact that Sir Matt Busby and Dennis Law (see page 36), world-class players, never had the experience of taking part in a Scottish League match.

The number of Scots attached to English Football League clubs has been consistently large. There were 362 in 1929, 258 in 1965, and although by 1975 this number had fallen to 198, no fewer than 82 of these were First Division players. The recent sharp fall has been caused by the tendency of clubs in the lower English divisions to prune professional staffs severely, and to concentrate their scouting efforts locally.

The Scots in England were curiously uneven in their distribution. Certain clubs relied heavily on them, with Sunderland and Preston North End traditionally well disposed. There were four Scots in the Sunderland cup-winning side of 1937 and seven in the Preston team which was successful the following year. On the other hand, for a thirty-year spell early in the present century West Bromwich Albion refused to employ a Scottish player, presumably as the result of an unhappy experience with an early Scots 'professor'.

London clubs tended to steer clear of Scots until comparatively recently, and only at Chelsea, with the presence of the aristocratic Alec Jackson and the tragic, plebeian Hughie Gallagher, was the Scottish influence really strong between the wars. Arsenal were not noted for their fondness for Scotsmen, but they did have Alec James (see page 36) who, with his rotund figure and absurdly baggy shorts, was the darling of the sports cartoonists of the late 1920s and '30s. In England, James was regarded as the archetype of the Scottish inside forward in the same way that Sir Harry Lauder was considered to be the quintessential Scottish entertainer; indeed the two were not infrequently bracketed together when 'Caledonia's favoured sons' were mentioned.

In the north of England, the number of Scots engaged in professional football was always appreciably higher, and around 1955 the Third Division North side, Accrington Stanley, regularly fielded as many as ten Scots and on at least four occasions an entirely Scottish team. When to the figures previously quoted are added the large number of Scots playing non-league football in England, it can be seen that the revenue earned from the English game was very substantial.

Scots in the F.A. Cup Finals

Scots players were not slow to take advantage of the magnificent setting for the F.A. Cup Final which Wembley Stadium, originally the Imperial Stadium, provided. The names of the scorers in cup finals read like a Scottish roll of honour. In 1924, in the second final at Wembley, Neil Harris became the first Scot to score there. In 1927 Hugh Ferguson scored the goal which beat Arsenal and gave Cardiff City and Wales the cup for the first and only time. Alec James scored for Arsenal when they won in 1930, and another wizard, Tim Dunn, scored one of Everton's three goals against Manchester City three years later. It is needless to catalogue all the Scots scorers over the years, but some goals stand out—for example, the penalty in the last minute of extra time in the 1938 final which George Mutch from Arbroath converted to give Preston North End the trophy after they had lost the year before. That was a memorable Wembley moment, as was the goal scored for Charlton by Chris Duffy, again in extra time, against Burnley in 1947. Duffy earned the unstinted gratitude of the crowd for preventing a replay of what even today, thirty-one years on, is still generally regarded as the poorest of post-war finals. In the 1953 final and the two subsequent ones, Scots scored in each, but mostly for the losing side. Manchester United's goals in 1963—two to David Herd, one to Denis Law—were cup-winners, as was Ian St John's for Liverpool against Leeds in 1965, when his goal beat one of Billy Bremner's.

Shots by Jimmy Robertson for Spurs and Eddie Kelly for Arsenal kept the Cup in London in 1967 and 1971, and the last Scottish scorer in a Wembley final to date is possibly the most remarkable of all: Ian Porterfield, a not particularly highly regarded player, with a not particularly highly regarded club, Sunderland, who in 1973 nevertheless defeated the red-hot favourites, Leeds. The match was an excellent example of Scotland's abiding contribution to English football, for of the twenty-two players on the field, no fewer than eight were Scots.

The Anglos in internationals

Inevitably, the Anglo-Scot loomed very large in Scottish international sides of the time. The 5-1 thrashing administered to England by the Wembley Wizards of 1928 was preceded by one of the most famous cartoons in Scottish football. The London train is shown leaving Glasgow with three disconsolate Home Scots players, Harkness, Dunn and Morton. The caption reads, 'The selectors might have given us another for a hand at solo'.

The thousands of followers who travelled south that year were happy enough that there had been eight Anglos in the winning team, but there exists always a curious love-hate relationship between the Scottish supporter and the English-based players in our national sides. The Anglos feel that they are more harshly judged, and certainly John White was by no means alone in feeling that Press and terracing set them higher standards than the home product.

From time to time there has been strong pressure to do without the Anglos and field an All-Tartan team. In the days before a Scottish team manager was appointed, it was a constant gibe that Anglos were included simply to justify the selectors' frequent jaunts south. Certainly the choice of such players as Black of Southampton in 1948 and Moir of Bolton Wanderers in 1950 for the matches against England at Hampden (both of which were lost) was difficult to comprehend. All-Tartan sides defeated England in 1925 and 1931, but if any proof were needed of the value of the Anglos, it can be found in comparing our results against England in international matches with our results in inter-league games. In full internationals we are entitled to use Scots playing in England, in inter-league matches we are restricted to players with Scottish clubs, and there is no doubt about which category produces better results for Scotland.

SCOTLAND	*v.*	ENGLAND
36	23 drawn	34

SCOTTISH LEAGUE	*v.*	FOOTBALL LEAGUE
18	14 drawn	40

In recent years a chief criticism of Anglo-Scots has been that they are unwilling to be disciplined by a team manager

Alec James (Arsenal)

Denis Law (Manchester United)

who has no English managerial experience. There is no doubt that gifted players, such as Bremner and Law, had a bad track record for on-field and off-field behaviour. They brought to the Scottish side, however, a unique combativeness which, while occasionally misplaced—perhaps often misplaced—was an invaluable quality. They were the players who, week in, week out, listened in English dressing-rooms to their team-mates' jeers about the quality of Scottish football. Once every year they had the chance to settle old scores and very often they took it.

Scottish footballers have been particularly esteemed in England for their fierce competitiveness and their creative flair. Paradoxically, their anarchical tendencies and reluctance to conform have on occasion enhanced their value in the tactics-ridden modern game.

Disastrously, from a Scottish point of view, the road south has almost always been a road of no return. There are few instances of a player, once having gone to England, returning to Scotland at anything approaching the height of his powers. The case of Billy Steel, the gifted international inside-forward who returned to Dundee from Derby County, is almost the only one which comes readily to mind.

Scottish players who have gone south have often subsequently expressed their bewilderment and occasional annoyance at the attitude of the Hampden crowds towards them, which, although well-meaning, has had unfortunate effects. Charlie Cooke, the thoughtful Chelsea veteran, puts it this way:

> "You go out at Hampden and before you know where you are you're dashing about mad all over the place, trying to make a name. You'd never dream of playing like that with your club in England, and if you had played like that you would never have been picked for Scotland in the first place. But the frenzy of the crowd gets to you and you can't help yourself."

The selection of a Scottish home player for the international side has always made his departure for England very likely, and since 1961 the abolition of the maximum wage in England has greatly increased that probability. Even Rangers and Celtic now find it extremely difficult to cling to a player who wants to move. The departure of Kenny Dalglish from Celtic to Liverpool in August 1977 is an outstanding example. Dalglish's move followed the transfers of Lou Macari to Manchester United and David Hay to Chelsea, and not even the resources of a great club like Celtic were proof against this appalling drain of skill and inventiveness.

Since the two clubs mentioned can almost always match English wages, it follows that money is not the sole attraction which England offers. Professional pride has something to do with it—the feeling that a player has not proved himself until he has been successful in the Football League, which is by repute the most competitive in the world. The outstanding achievement of Celtic in 1967, when for the first time the European Cup came to Britain, went some way to show that home-based players could compete successfully with the best in the world. There will have to be other such triumphs soon, if the Scottish game is to remain credible.

Many of the leading Scottish players are with Rangers and Celtic. The more sensitive of them dislike the religious rancour which disfigures the Scottish game and, quite apart from financial considerations, prefer the more urbane and relaxed atmosphere of the south. The strong Scottish element in league football has caused problems for England at international level in the same way that the influx of overseas cricketers has damaged her Test prospects in the 1970s.

In the concentration on the Scots player in England, one tends to lose sight of our contribution to their game at managerial level. In the last twenty years most of the highly successful managers in England have been Scots—the roll includes Sir Matt Busby, Tommy Docherty of Derby County, Bill Shankly, Eddie McCreadie of Chelsea, and Dave Mackay.

If the Scots have done well by English football, they have done equally well from it. In the *Football Who's Who* of 1935, several Anglo-Scots listed their recreations as motoring, at a time when very few working-men aspired to car ownership. The game offered money, it offered fame of a kind, however temporary. From the heavy industrial areas the aspirants flocked south.

Over the years the recruiting areas shifted. Of the 362 Football League Scots in 1929, the major part came from the three great mining areas of Lanarkshire, Ayrshire and Fife. By the 1960s the geographical locations had changed markedly. Ayrshire as a source of recruitment had virtually dried up, and the flow from Lanarkshire was markedly reduced. The cities of Aberdeen and Edinburgh were going a long way to balance this falling off.

During the Easter holidays most English First Division clubs test out little groups of Scottish schoolboys to find if someone may possibly have the skill, the stamina and the mental toughness to become a successful professional footballer. Somewhere there may be another Billy Liddell, who went south at fourteen to become a legendary Liverpool footballer and a highly successful accountant. It is the Scottish sporting equivalent of 'From Log Cabin to White House'.

The success of the Anglos is a source of legitimate pride to us, but it is a pride tinged with the melancholy reflection that on any Saturday afternoon, the home-based supporter can see very few of the men who made possible World Cup Argentina in 1978.

Conditions of Service

TO the man on the terracing, who paid his two shillings each Saturday, the Scottish professional footballer of the late 1950s appeared to have an enviable life. He was being paid, and paid above industrial level, for doing what he would probably have done for amusement. If he reached the top of his profession he could increasingly expect to travel widely, and he was the subject of flattering and sometimes hysterical adulation.

The prospect did not look quite so inviting to those involved in the game, and some of the grievances of the players had been set out in the *Scottish Football Players' Union Journal* of October 1951. There was nothing unusual in the claim which was being advanced for an improvement in wages. More interesting was the recitation of the other disadvantages under which professional players laboured on both sides of the border.

The main target was the contract which the player signed with the club and which bound him to that club for the duration of his playing career if the club so desired. Any appeal which the player might make against this situation was to a management committee of the League; it could be plausibly argued that he was thus appealing to the very people who were putting him in his original position. A player who hesitated about re-signing, or declined to do so, could be placed on the transfer list at an inflated fee. It is true that such a fee could be, and often was, reduced drastically on appeal, but the process was time consuming, and in the nature of things a professional footballer has no time to squander. There were non-league clubs to which a player could go in defiance of League edicts, but these were all in England, so a Scots player had to contemplate a separation from his family at a period of severe housing shortage.

Clubs could play off the Scottish League and Scottish

Football Association against the player by placing him on the open-to-transfer list with one body and the retained list with the other. Footballers were particularly enraged with their miserly share of transfer fees agreed between the clubs. The maximum sum which they could claim within the laws of football was £750, if they had completed five years' satisfactory service with the transferring club. Since £30,000 transfer fees were commonplace by the mid-1950s, this meant that the player received something in the region of 3 per cent of the money exchanged by the clubs. The system bred deceit, and there were cases where large sums were paid to players for the alleged purchase of their old cars, to encourage them to change quarters. Occasionally the father of a young player would be taken on to the club's books as a scout, and paid promptly so long as he obeyed instructions never to recommend a player.

It must be said again that professional players in the Scottish First Division of 1951/52, making between £10 and £14 per week, were doing well by the standards of most of their watchers. They were not being adequately paid, however, for crowds at Scottish football were abnormally high in the ten years following the war. In the 1956/57 season Rangers played to an average home gate of 36,000, and although this was far and away the best attendance, Hearts averaged 24,500, Celtic 18,000 and Hibernian the same. A top-liner, appearing in a variety show at the Alhambra or Empire theatre in Glasgow at that time, could confidently expect to be paid a three-figure sum weekly.

The players were ever conscious of the brief span in which they could make money. The average length of time that a player spent in top-class football was calculated to be just over eight years. He had to contend not only with injury and loss of form but with such imponderables as changes of management. His style might be unacceptable to a new manager, although his performance was unimpaired. In those clubs—and there were many—where the manager was simply an office boy for the Board, a player could easily lose his place by falling foul of a director or a director's wife.

In the edition of the *Scottish Football Players' Union Journal* already quoted, the Management Committee alluded to a manifest injustice which incensed footballers. Professional cricketers had an existence which was every bit as precarious and even more poorly paid, but at the end of their career was the great rainbow in the shape of a benefit. This was tax free and, even before the First World War, had often run into four figures. Dr W. G. Grace, who in theory was an amateur, received over £8,000 from testimonials got up by his devoted admirers.

The footballer could look for no such windfall. The club could, but did not have to, pay him a benefit of £750 maximum, less tax, at the end of five years. The distinction was stated in the case of Reed *v.* Seymour, decided in the House of Lords in 1927. The Lords held that Seymour, a Kent cricketer, need not pay tax on the proceeds of a benefit match because the money realised was in the nature of a personal gift. On the other hand, the benefit paid to a professional footballer was a payment made by the football club out of their funds as part of their contractual obligations. It was to take footballers in Scotland almost forty years to realise that if a testimonial match were organised and run independently of the employing club, then tax would not be payable on the sum received.

The more intelligent a player was, the more difficult he found it to put in his day as a full-time footballer. The amount of physical training that a player could do in a day was obviously limited, and the afternoons yawned before many. Golf was a popular pastime, encouraged by the clubs, and often no serious objection was raised if the player took a part-time job, provided there was no conflict of duty. In the 1950s several Scottish international players worked as assistants in a big Glasgow clothing store, and several ghosted columns for the sports pages of newspapers. The market for players to conclude profitable advertising deals was and remains limited in Scotland, and at the time referred to there was no equivalent of the lucrative endorsements which linked Denis Compton with Brylcreem and Stanley

Matthews (surprisingly, since he was a non-smoker) with Craven 'A'.

It would be quite inaccurate to depict the clubs as universally hard and grasping employers. Often their attitude towards their players was kindly and paternalistic. Instances are easily found in the club minute-books of players being extricated from scrapes and financial morasses. Kilmarnock arranged for a player to be given an advance to prevent a threatened eviction; St Mirren made provision for nursing-home care for a player who succumbed to melancholia, and the player's family was looked after as well.

Supervision could be stern. When St Mirren allowed a famous player of the late 1920s, Dunky Walker, to become involved in the running of a pub, a decision contrary to established club policy, they appear soon to have regretted their decision. There is an entry in the St Mirren minutes of November 1922 which records the Board's intention of engaging a private detective to follow D. Walker on account of his 'disgraceful behaviour'. Rather disappointingly, Walker was either too smart for the detective or was living a life of blameless virtue, for the investigator was soon removed from the case. The life of the professional player would have been tightly circumscribed if the clubs had had their way. There was a constant battle, normally good-humoured, with those footballers who sought to evade club discipline as public schoolboys were apt to try to break bounds.

The end of the retain-and-transfer system

It had long been thought that the retain-and-transfer system, as operated in football, would not survive the first determined attack made on it in a court of law, and so it proved. The onslaught was made first in England, and the result has had a profound effect on the career prospects of the Scottish professional footballer. In 1959, George Eastham of Newcastle United wished to move south to Arsenal for personal reasons. His club refused to contemplate such a move and

Eastham raised an action which was to become a test case for the professional footballers of Great Britain.

As many lawyers had predicted, in the summer of 1963 the High Court decided in his favour. They found for him on two issues. The rules governing the retain-and-transfer system were *ultra vires*, in that the powers were not conferred on the limited company (Newcastle United) by its Memorandum and Articles of Association. The second *ratio decidendi* was that the retain-and-transfer system was unlawful because in effect it was in restraint of trade.

This has led to the system of option contracts, whereby a player is signed for one or two years, and the club has an option to renew his contract for the same period. The option must be for the same period of time, and on terms at least as favourable, unless by mutual agreement between club and player. If the club does not wish to take up its option at the end of the initial period, the player is free to sign for another club without any transfer being required.

Appeal is still in the first instance to the Management Committee of the respective leagues, but beyond that, either club or player can appeal to the Independent Tribunal. This consists of one representative from the Football League (Scottish) and one member of the Professional Footballers' Association, and it is chaired by the Chairman of the Joint Negotiating Committee.

The effect in Scotland

Scottish League football clubs who wished to keep the services of their best players now found another difficulty. Provision was soon made by the Football League that a 10 per cent levy would be imposed on all transfer fees above £500. Of this 10 per cent, half was payable to the Football League and the other half to the player being transferred, provided he had not demanded a transfer or, through misconduct, virtually forced his club to get rid of him. Although the two largest Scottish clubs, Celtic and Rangers, might match English wages, the top Scots player could now gain a substantial capital sum by moving to England, for he would make £7,500 on a £150,000 transfer fee. He could invest this money and let it work for him, an important consideration in such a risky occupation as professional football.

The outcome of the Eastham decision for Scotland has been finally to make it impossible to match over a prolonged period the financial benefits which would accrue to a player if he moved south. There is a certain rough justice in the knowledge that when players are granted freedom to negotiate their own contracts (very near at the time of writing), English clubs will be in the same disadvantageous position *vis-à-vis* Europe. It is through the individual negotiating his contract, rather than through normal trade union solidarity, that the lot of the professional footballer is most likely to be dramatically improved.

The individual player is not in a strong position if he attempts to withdraw his labour. His club can refuse him training facilities, and the longer he goes without playing, the more his transfer value depreciates. A club has several courses of action against a discontented player. It can immediately drop him to the reserves, thus cutting his income drastically. It can hint that he is a disciplinary problem (this assumes that the club wants to keep the player). The alternatives are to transfer the player, or to pay him more. Some clubs, Celtic in particular, make it club policy never to retain a discontented player. With the larger clubs, where the practice of negotiating individual contracts is more prevalent, it is possible to allay the player's discontent by paying him more than his colleagues, but this course has obvious difficulties. It is hard to keep such an arrangement secret for long, and in any case the end of the player's militancy may become very marked.

For many years, but especially since 1970, the Scottish Professional Footballers' Association has made an effort to have an articulate representative player in each club, who will put the Association's viewpoint to Boards and managers—trenchantly if necessary. Almost all clubs afford facilities for the S.P.F.A. secretary to come to the grounds to speak to players, and to exhibit notices and proposals.

There has been a lack of a militant tradition among the players, most of whom realise that clubs are semi-permanently in a precarious financial position and that they are already in some cases paying unrealistic wages which can only be met because directors are prepared to underwrite the running expenses of the club. (Here it might be said that the sums of money which are now allocated by the League from the money given by football pools promoters have lessened the financial burden on individual directors and boards collectively.) There has been only one well-authenticated instance of players refusing to take the field when instructed to do so. The club concerned was Celtic, the time was the last decade of the past century, and the occasion was not a financial quarrel, but the wish of certain of the Celtic players to have a reporter excluded from the press-box on the grounds that his criticism of them had been unjustly severe.

The two outstanding club sides in Scotland, Celtic and Rangers, have always treated players' organisations such as the Scottish Professional Footballers' Association with suspicion and hostility. Their normal method of combating such bodies has been to pay players well, rather than risk genuine union involvement. They were able to pursue this policy successfully, since the absence of a maximum wage eliminated competition from English clubs for their players, and because, in the restricted field of Scottish football, their rate of playing success was very high, so that bonuses became almost an integral part of the weekly wage.

The S.P.F.A. has found in recent years that it can gain a certain amount of support from the players of whichever Old Firm club is not doing particularly well. Only now is the union making a determined attack on such anomalies as the fact that the contracts for full-time and part-time players are precisely the same, and the unfair distinction which the Inland Revenue makes between benefits awarded to professional footballers and those given to cricketers. The Association has also been successful in gaining for players who have been summoned before the Scottish Football Association the right to be represented by the Secretary of the S.P.F.A. It also intends, at the first opportunity, to test in the law courts the right of the Scottish Football Association to pass sentences of suspension which have the effect of depriving a full-time professional footballer of his living.

Footballers are not an easy group for a union to represent, and in many respects the S.P.F.A. faces the same difficulties as does the actors' union, Equity. There is the same abundance of entrants, many with more enthusiasm than real ability, and there are not enough places even for those with real ability. Because of the fiercely competitive nature of the profession, general wages are low but rewards at the top are very high, and the player who has achieved personal playing success feels little need to identify with his less fortunate colleagues. There is a much higher degree of mobility among professional footballers than among cricketers, where associations of twenty years with the one county are common. This fluidity means that footballers are not often with a club long enough to acquire the position of elder statesmen and spokesmen for their team-mates, whereas in cricket there is the recognised, though sometimes unpaid, position of senior professional.

For these reasons, it seems unlikely that in the immediate future the Scottish Professional Footballers' Association will be able to acquire a position of real strength in relation to the Scottish Football Association or the Scottish League.

In the cynical world of industrial negotiations, a players' union has no real bargaining power, even when brought under the umbrella of the Transport and General Workers' Union. The public does not have to watch football and could contemplate a prolonged strike with much more equanimity than could the strikers, who dare not risk allowing the public to form other amusement habits on Saturday afternoons. The well-orchestrated and highly organised attempt by the T.G.W.U. to prevent the Scotland international against Chile from taking place in June 1977 completely failed to achieve its purpose.

Discipline and punishment of players is another matter. It was not so much that under the old system injustice was done. It was more negative than that—justice was not seen to be done. It is virtually certain that never again will a footballer receive a *sine die* suspension which removes him from the game for an indefinite period, perhaps forever. Officially, players who were under suspension were not supposed to be paid; that too will be found unacceptable to modern thinking.

Even with these improvements the professional player will not lead anything other than a highly fraught and uneasy life. His skill, transient and overwhelmingly dependent on his colleagues, is all he has to offer. Week by week, in the widest variety of climatic conditions and against all sorts of physical and mental intimidation, he submits himself to rigorous and merciless public scrutiny. It is an ordeal that few of us need face, and an excellent reason for according our respect and affection to those who must do so.

Even in recent times the Scottish professional has been disturbed by seeming injustice. A lavish bonus structure on a poor basic wage may suit a young bachelor very well, but a mature married player in mid- or late career finds it unsatisfactory to receive a wage which may fluctuate wildly from week to week. The influx in the early 1960s of such overseas players as Finn Dossing, Mogens Berg and Lennart Wing of Dundee United, Kai Johansen, Carl Bertelsen and Erik Sorensen of Morton, caused some heart-searching. They were signed as amateurs from Scandinavian football, and could therefore be paid substantial lump sums. They were entertaining players, but had no long-term commitment to Scottish football. At the end of two or three years they were free to negotiate with European clubs and virtually make their own terms.

The payment, the just payment, of players in a team game is more difficult to resolve satisfactorily than the payment of a top-line golfer or tennis player, whose price is what his current form commands. In a football team, Matthews or Baxter or Law is highly dependent on the fetching and carrying of team-mates who may be his inferiors, but without their services he cannot properly put his skill to account. The financial reward of players will inevitably remain a contentious area.

The Last Whistle Blows

TODAY's professional footballer is no longer automatically tomorrow's publican. He may be a hotelier, run a sports shop, represent a large firm as a salesman, revert to the career as accountant or dentist which he forsook temporarily. Yet for many players the end of their playing days, though clearly foreseen, comes as a traumatic shock. At the height of their physical powers and mental vigour, at approximately thirty-five years of age, they can no longer employ the only skills they possess. If the discarded footballer has been a full-time player since the age of sixteen, the outside world may well seem bleak and strange. It is hardly surprising therefore that many seek to keep a toehold in the world of professional football by serving a club in some administrative capacity.

The player as manager

The job of a football manager is a complex one, calling for many differing skills, yet over the last twenty years Scottish clubs have been prepared to offer this post to candidates who have no qualification other than that of having been players of repute, which is rather like offering the conductorship of the London Symphony Orchestra to the most technically proficient musician. The smaller the club, the more diverse the manager's range of accomplishments must be, yet until very recently there was absolutely no formal job-training.

It is difficult to quantify success in football managership. Indeed since the 'manufacturing process', the winning of matches, is outside the direct physical control of the manager, many would argue that success is based upon luck, pure and simple. There are sufficient examples of managers who have been consistently successful with clubs of different potential to allow us to believe that there are certain qualities which are likely to produce success in a manager. Such examples include Herbert Chapman, who led Huddersfield Town and Arsenal to domination of English football in the 1920s and '30s; Jock Stein, who had successes with Dunfermline Athletic, Hibernian and Celtic; and Eddie Turnbull with Queen's Park, Aberdeen and Hibernian.

The ex-footballer turned manager requires considerable versatility. To his players he must be psychologist and master-tactician, though in the latter area a few strokes of luck can acquire for him at least a temporary reputation. He must be a good judge of a player and, perhaps even more vital, a good judge of a scout. He has to refrain from signing a gifted player with serious character flaws, resisting the temptation of thinking that he will be able to handle this man when others have failed. Increasingly in the modern game, he has to be a public relations officer for his club. It is interesting that even where such a post has been separately and officially created, men such as Jock Stein of Celtic and Willie Waddell of Rangers have insisted on being spokesmen for the club in announcements of major importance concerning the playing side.

It is essential that the modern manager should be able to establish and maintain good relations with the Press and broadcasting media. To do this he must be fairly articulate, and he has a difficult task, for the interests of the media and the manager will often be antipathetic. In his dealings with his own Board, a manager must exercise a high degree of diplomacy, and be quick to realise where power lies with individual directors. Alternatively, he must achieve such a degree of playing success as to defy removal.*

* There has been a marked increase in the severity of attitudes shown by Boards towards managers, perhaps partially accounted for by the fact that the manager really does manage much more often now in such areas as team selection. Yet, making all allowances for this, the frequency with which some clubs change managers borders on the grotesque. In the twenty years which followed the Second World War, managers tended to stay longer, with First Division clubs at any rate. They acquired essential epithets in the Press—'shrewd', 'genial', 'pipe-smoking'. Occasionally a manager achieved the triple distinction of being shrewd, genial and pipe-smoking. Falkirk were inseparably associated with Tully Craig, Motherwell with John Hunter, Clyde with Pat Travers, Raith Rovers with Bert Herdman. In a situation of managerial stability, these sides performed perceptibly better than they have in their more frenzied recent history. Most managerial changes betoken an admission by a board of directors of the fallibility of their own powers of selection, nothing more.

The manager of one of the smaller clubs may well have to combine secretarial work with playing supervision, and it is very uncommon for one man to be adept in both fields. With the bigger concerns, the manager is free to concentrate on developing the football skills of his players, leaving the secretarial tasks to others.

There is no clinching reason why the manager should himself have been an outstanding professional footballer, and indeed this used not to be the case. Such highly successful managers as Herbert Chapman of Arsenal, Bill Struth of Rangers and Willie McCartney of Heart of Midlothian and Hibernian had either played no football at top level or so little that it hardly counted. The advent of the modern track-suited manager changed things drastically. Although a brand of super-coaches, rather than managers, emerged in Europe, England was very slow to follow this lead, and Scotland slower still.

At the beginning of season 1976/77, of the twenty-four leading clubs in Scotland, all were managed by ex-players, and all but two of these had performed with distinction during their playing careers. Incredible though it seems, there is still no formal training for management in Scotland for the player who is approaching the end of his active career and is contemplating switching from dressing-room to office. The giants of the Scottish game, Celtic, Hearts, Hibernian and Rangers, have often sent one of their own past players of distinction to manage a smaller club for on-the-job experience. In some cases he has occupied a subordinate position with a larger club. Thus Jock Stein of Celtic served his managerial apprenticeship with Dunfermline Athletic, Scot Symon of Rangers started as manager of East Fife, and Tommy Walker of Hearts had a spell as assistant manager of Chelsea. All three ended up as managers of the clubs with which they had made their reputations as players.

For the last twenty-five years, then, the primary qualifications for appointment as manager have been skill and renown as a player. The importance of these in a manager can be underestimated; players tend to despise those connected

Billy McNeill, an outstanding Celtic captain and now manager of Aberdeen

with the game who have not been exposed to the pressures of top-class football, and it is hard for a manager who has never earned his living as a player to command the respect of his playing staff. He must be regarded as a 'player's man', even though he is also a salaried employee with a responsibility towards his board of directors.

In the summer of 1973 an event occurred which may prove

to be significant for the Scottish footballers of the future who wish to stay in the game when their playing days are over. The first formal training course for managers was instituted at the St Helen's College of Technology in Lancashire. This was an attempt to give the new or trainee manager a thorough grounding in the most important aspects of his job. Among the topics discussed were the psychology of coaching, how to handle individual grievances, contract law (there were six lectures on this), fund-raising, crowd-control, public relations and ground maintenance. Managers were also taught how to read balance sheets.

The course tutor, Mr Gerry Burrows, offered this definition of the role of a manager: "I see the role of the football manager as being a blend of executive and supervisor. He needs skill at both ends of the managerial ladder." It would be a logical development if Scottish clubs were to send present and aspiring managers on such a course, rather than attempt to set up one at Scottish level. An analogous situation obtains in coaching, where many Scottish players, having taken the S.F.A. coaching certificate, also sit for the qualification offered by the F.A., possession of which increases their chances of jobs abroad.

It has to be said that there is very little incentive for players to arm themselves with coaching certificates as the opportunities for employment are very few. Schools have set their faces resolutely against the professional coach (unless the player happens also to be a schoolmaster), and there are nothing like the number of jobs abroad which are open to the county cricketer, for example, during the English winter. Despite all uncertainties and discouragements, each managerial vacancy evokes a stream of applications from those who will brave any perils to stay directly involved in the game.

The Flawed Hero

INTERNATIONAL matches between Scotland and England have been going on now for over a hundred years, with Scotland having slightly the better of the exchanges. The style of the two national sides has, in an interesting way, reflected the supposed characteristics of their peoples. English sides have tended to be phlegmatic, disciplined, instructed, while the Scots have relied heavily on mood and feats of individual brilliance. The result has tended to be that England have seldom achieved greatness but almost never fall below a level of decent competence, while the Scots see-saw dizzily between heights and depths of attainment.

English and Scots fans have chosen to idolise very different players. In general, Englishmen have tended to applaud the 'good-image' type of professional footballer, the man who has played for many years, has been a good ambassador for his country at international level, and has avoided public scandal. It is almost essential that he be a good team man. An apparent exception, Sir Stanley Matthews, perhaps the most brilliant individualist that British football has ever produced, could be pardoned because his life-style was extremely conformist during his playing career.

Other English idols were Billy Wright, clean-cut, personable, dedicated to personal fitness (with the additional advantage of having married one of a trio of wholesome English girl singers, the Beverley Sisters), and his successor in the England captaincy, Bobby Moore. Both men had the much-prized quality of consistency. Wright indeed achieved the almost incredible feat of playing in 105 of the first 108 international matches in which England took part immediately after the Second World War. When his playing days were over, he maintained his conservative image by becoming manager of Arsenal F.C., very much the establishment club.

Bobby Moore of West Ham United was even more the very model of a modern professional footballer. Tall, fair-haired, pleasant-looking, he epitomised English football for much of the 1960s and early '70s. His life at times appeared almost to parody those sporting stories so beloved of boys' magazines. Thus, when he was involved in the celebrated case of the stolen bracelet in a Colombian hotel immediately before the World Cup finals in Mexico in 1970, there was general indignation and disbelief in England. Bobby was patently guiltless, his followers thought, and the whole incident could only have been contrived by sinister dagoes who wished to diminish his effectiveness in the forthcoming competition. These things happened, they knew, because they had often read of them in the *Rover*, *Hotspur* or even, at a more exalted level, in John Buchan. When inquiries were made, the Englishman would be completely vindicated. And so it proved.

The Scottish players for whom the Scots fans have reserved their special adoration have often proved to be different in their personalities and attitudes from those just cited. It is true that some conventionally 'good guys' have been enshrined in the affections of the game's patrons. One thinks of John Thomson of Celtic, a brilliant goalkeeper whose tragically early death on the playing field ensured that his memory would flourish more than it might otherwise have done. Tommy Walker of Hearts (see page 17), a most courteous man on and off the field, has a special place in the memory of Scottish fans. It is a curious quirk of the Scots character, however, that absolute idolatry has often been reserved for troublesome and troubled players, and to these the nation has opened its heart. In the 1920s such a player was Hughie Gallacher of Airdrie and Newcastle United, and in recent times the trend has been exemplified in the cases of Jim Baxter of Rangers and Jimmy Johnstone of Celtic.

Jim Baxter

Jim Baxter (see page 61) would have few challengers for the

title of the most compellingly artistic Scottish footballer since 1945. He was an aristocrat sprung from a Fife mining village, lean to the point of emaciation. Throughout his career he was known as 'Slim Jim', even when the name had long ceased to be apposite. He first came to light with Raith Rovers in 1958, but had no intention of remaining long with the Fife club. He had been advised in this by his veteran team-mate, Willie McNaught, whose sixteen years at Starks' Park had brought him a handful of international caps, universally good press notices, and very little money. When Rangers beckoned, Baxter was quick to respond.

At once he imposed his individual brand of cool elegance upon his new club. Hurry was not in his vocabulary. A leisurely killing of the ball, a contemptuous, languid survey of the field, and then swiftly a pass would lance its way to an unmarked team-mate. It was a formula which worked well at all levels; his skill stood up against the most intensive European competition and he was undoubtedly a player of world class. Official recognition of this came when he was selected to play for the Rest of the World against England in 1963. Even towards the end of his remarkably brief career—brief given the pace at which he played—he conveyed the impression of mentally dominating his opponents.

His attitude towards his employers was even more remarkable than his skill as a player. Above all other clubs, Arsenal in England and Rangers in Scotland had surrounded themselves with a quasi-religious mystique which for many years would serve them well, but in the long run prove disastrous. Baxter was the man who, almost single-handed, dispelled this aura in the case of Rangers. Certain that he possessed greater playing ability than any of his colleagues, he was not to be impressed by the marble staircases and trophy rooms of Ibrox. Unlike almost every Old Firm player of his era, he was never a jersey-player, that is, one who, for emotive or cultural reasons, would almost have been prepared to play for nothing for the club of his loyalty. Baxter was the perfect mercenary; the club were due his best endeavours and almost always got them, but that did not mean that he had to subscribe to the underlying pomp or philosophy. He dragged his feet at conventional training, whether at club or international level, knowing perfectly well that exercises designed to build up muscle and stamina were not going to be of particular assistance to him. He was quite prepared to socialise with opposition players, and for several years one of his most frequent companions was Pat Crerand of Celtic, something which did not meet with universal approval at Ibrox.

He was very much of his generation, typifying as he did the highly prized quality of 'cool' and a readiness to cock a snook at authority. His mode of dress would have induced apoplexy in former Rangers' managers, particularly Mr William Struth, but no one could deny Baxter's flair or sense of occasion. His most serious injury, a leg-break, occurred in Vienna when he was playing the game of his career and at a point in the match when he knew that his efforts had pulled Rangers through, so that his departure from the pitch on a stretcher had a certain Nelsonian quality about it.

He experienced great success too as a Scotland player, especially when playing before the highly partisan and not always perceptive Scottish crowds at Hampden. Yet it is appropriate that the match which more than any other endeared him to his countrymen was the 1967 international at Wembley when, although he was in the winning Scottish side, his display was tactically inept in the extreme. A good Scotland team was coasting to victory at 2-0 and then 3-1, with the chance to turn undoubted superiority into tangible terms. Most Scots saw the humiliation of England in a 4-1 or 5-1 score. Not so Baxter. His idea was to keep possession, to bait the English with short, square passes, to make little or no attempt to attack further. He treated the England side as a matador the bull. The Scottish fans on the Wembley terracing were delighted at this display of bravado, for which they undoubtedly used the Glasgow word 'gallusness'. Baxter's plan had only one defect. It did not work. An England side two goals behind and with two players crippling along came back to 3-2, and were not very far away from the eventual saving of the match. Yet few of the fans were inclined to censure Baxter, for he had shown up the English on their own ground, and that might almost have been a worthwhile price to pay for losing the game.

His presence in the international side guaranteed at one and the same time that Scotland would occasionally perform brilliantly and would rarely, if ever, play the same way in two successive matches. Rangers would have kept him, but his desire to move south, and his ever more open subversion of much of what the club had stood for, made this impossible. Predictably, in the more disciplined context of English football, he achieved comparatively little. Sunderland at least got most of their money back from Nottingham Forest, but he was a very bad buy for the latter club. When he returned to Rangers for a second spell, he was tubby and lethargic. Occasionally flashes of the old brilliance would remind crowds that they were in the presence of a once truly great player, but such flashes became less and less frequent. He retired when he should have been able to continue playing for another five years, but he was the stuff of legend.

There are thousands of supporters who have his stride, his passing and shooting, and his petulance, etched vividly on their memories, although they have forgotten the style and deportment of many of his colleagues who were model professionals. One last anecdote may fix him in the place he holds in the collective Scottish football folklore. In a match against Uruguay at Hampden in 1962, a brawl developed, in the course of which a Scottish player, with no very great malice, took a light-hearted kick at the referee. The identity of the culprit has never been established beyond doubt, nor is it likely to be, but most Scottish supporters suspected, and many half-hoped, that it might have been Jim Baxter. It was 'the kind of thing Jim might do'.

Jimmy Johnstone

Given his physical appearance, it was impossible that Jimmy Johnstone (see page 61) could ever be one of the more anonymous professional footballers. A mere five foot four inches in height, frail in build, with all his vitality seemingly drained to a thatch of fiery red hair, he would have been a kenspeckle figure on the football field, even if he had not been one of the most original talents of his time. Skill was his stock-in-trade, that and an amount of courage that was altogether disproportionate to his size. Johnstone was one of the bravest players of his day; far from seeking to evade the physical challenge of much weightier opponents, he positively gloried in seeking it out. Indeed, his virtue of courage had a darker side, the occasional crude and blatant act of uncontrolled aggression. In the early stages of his career he got away with much which would not have passed uncondemned in a more robust player.

He was essentially a one-club player and his background was not dissimilar to that of Jim Baxter. He came from the housing-estate of Viewpark in Lanarkshire, an anonymous area that had once been connected with coal and is still connected, increasingly tenuously, with steel. When he signed on as a ball-boy at Parkhead he weighed exactly seven stones. Later, as a result of a toughening-up course, he increased his weight to just over nine stones, but was unable to add one cubit to his stature.

From his earliest appearances in top-class football, Johnstone revealed an ability to cover the ground at tremendous speed with a peculiar scuttling motion which earned him the nickname of 'The Flying Flea'. For much of his career there was a tendency to undervalue him in Scotland. Season after season at international level he had to be content to fill in occasionally for his fellow pocket-sized winger, Willie Henderson of Rangers. English critics were inclined to dismiss his performances as being achieved against Scottish clubs whose defences, in some cases, were of dubious quality. His true stature was not recognised throughout Britain until the European Cup semi-final of 1970, when both at Leeds and in Glasgow he tormented almost beyond endurance the very capable English international, Terry Cooper of Leeds United.

Jim Baxter (Rangers)

Jimmy Johnstone (Celtic)

Throughout his career Johnstone had two great obstacles to surmount. One was his thoroughly unreliable temperament. It is not enough to say that a winger of his skill would inevitably be subjected to rough treatment by opposing defenders and that retaliation was likewise inevitable. There are sufficient examples of even more skilled players than Johnstone—Stanley Matthews of Blackpool, Tom Finney of Preston North End, Gordon Smith of Hibernian—who were able to take such abuse in their stride and give their riposte in the most effective football manner, the making and scoring of goals. On at least two occasions when Johnstone was sent off, it would be hard to say that he was on the receiving end of the incident which immediately preceded his dismissal. He had many passages of arms with his manager at Celtic Park, Jock Stein, and was not slow to make his disapproval publicly evident when on occasions he was substituted during the course of a match.

He was a player of great natural gifts and some culpable weaknesses. He had a swerve that a rugby three-quarter would have envied, and a marvellous burst of pace over twenty yards or so. His shot was surprisingly strong, and for a man of his height, he scored many more goals with his head than would have seemed likely. But he came to senior football a notoriously bad corner-kicker, and left it without having made any perceptible improvement. All too often his game seemed to rely on supreme bursts of individuality rather than any real tactical flair; for much of his career he appeared to imagine that goals could frequently be scored from an angle of 90 degrees.

I mentioned two obstacles. The second, which he tried most bravely to overcome, was a terrible fear of flying. It is hard to overemphasise the additional strain that such a fear must have imposed upon a player with a club which had such an unbroken record of European success as Celtic had in the five years after 1967. Jock Stein turned this morbid terror brilliantly to account when he promised Johnstone that he would excuse him from the return match with Red Star, Yugoslavia, in the European Cup match of 1968 if the little winger helped to build up a big enough lead in the first leg in Glasgow. Johnstone went out to play a masterly game and to score two of the five goals which rendered his trip to Yugoslavia unnecessary.

He came into the Scottish international side as Jim Baxter's star was in decline, although the two were several times team-mates in a Scottish jersey. Johnstone had his moments against other countries, becoming one of the very few Scottish players since the war to score two goals against England at Hampden Park, and one of the even fewer who have done this and finished up on the losing side. He was not receptive to any patterned plan, however, and acquired the reputation of being difficult to play with because he was almost impossible to read. He was embroiled with trainers, managers and officials at international level, who perhaps did not always handle their difficult star with the necessary tact and encouragement. Scotland chose him for the national side eighteen times, yet he may well be best remembered for an escapade at Largs while the national side was preparing for a European tour. Having broken team bounds at night, he was swept out to sea in a small boat, and although the incident had comical overtones, the ending could well have been grim.

Eventually the little winger who, in Jock Stein's words, had given more trouble than the rest of the staff put together, was allowed to leave Parkhead and seek a career in England with Sheffield United. There, he was perhaps the most predictable failure of recent years. He was so much a product of industrial Lanarkshire that he could have no lasting success away from the club which he had so frequently flouted.

Jimmy Johnstone was a very different type of player from Jim Baxter, but they had much in common. Despite their shortcomings, which the crowds realised perfectly well, they attracted the fierce loyalty of their supporters. Sometimes those supporters manifested this love in an unfair way. Rangers players who were expending three times the effort of Baxter would be cruelly barracked, while the slim Adonis strolled through a match physically and vocally unscathed. At Parkhead, colleagues of Johnstone, who had twice his football acumen, would be savagely hounded for the most trivial error, whereas Johnstone, even below form—and few players were ever more off on an off-day—was beyond censure. Both players were very much their own men. Moreover, they were the men their admirers, huddled together on the rainswept terracing, would dearly have liked to be. They personified the mute revolt of the industrial Scot against the appalling surroundings in which he was called upon to spend his working and social life.

The Violent Fan

AN inhabitant of Newcastle, Manchester, Birmingham, Wolverhampton or London, taking a word-association test, would be very likely to link 'Scots football fan' with the adjectives 'drunken', 'foul-mouthed' and 'belligerent'. All these cities have suffered under the visitations of Scottish supporters, as indeed has Barcelona. The reputation of the tartan grotesques who swarm across the border is akin to that of the janissaries who sustained the Ottoman Empire.

Sociologists have found the behaviour of football fans an almost inexhaustible seam in which to quarry. The vast majority of the Scottish travelling support comes from the industrial central lowlands of Scotland, one of the most depressed and deprived areas of the developed countries of the world. There is a real pathos in the ferocity with which the fans seek to flaunt the superiority of things Scottish, a trait which is literally pathetic in that it only serves to demonstrate more clearly the appalling spiritual poverty of the background from which they spring.

Their fathers and grandfathers came from the huddled tenements of Glasgow, Greenock, Clydebank and Paisley, from the dingy, two-storey houses of industrial Lanarkshire. The characteristics of the housing of those generations were the common close, the stairhead lavatory and the single cold-water tap. Real hunger and constant unemployment were their everyday companions. Until approximately 1960 there was, however, little record of violence on the comparatively infrequent trips made out of Scotland.

Scots only travelled in great numbers for the biennial match with England at Wembley. There was much dressing-up in tartan scarves and tammies by men who would have fainted with embarrassment had they been so garbed on any other day in their lives. 'Scots Wha Hae' was sung in victory, 'The Bonnie Wells o' Wearie' in defeat, but the occasion was essentially light-hearted and, in the strict sense, sporting. Large-scale and frequent crowd violence has been a creation of the 1960s. Its perpetrators are the generation who have been removed from the horrifying housing conditions of such areas as the Gorbals and Anderston in Glasgow, to the equally horrifying featureless housing schemes which have appeared on the outskirts of the old-established towns and cities of the central belt. Such areas are for the most part mere sleeping-places, without good shops, pubs, cinemas or any of the entertainment facilities which make life tolerable in an industrial society. With all their staggering defects as places in which to live, areas such as Anderston and Gorbals did engender a certain kinship which the Barlanarks, Easterhouses and Drumchapels have failed to re-create.

The Scottish supporter's love of football has been turned against him in the past. He knew and understood the game—when well played it was for many on the terracing the only art form which they would ever encounter. The emotional response of a Rangers supporter of the 1950s to a particularly skilled piece of combined play by his side—"Fuckin' poetry"—contains a sharp truth under the crudity. For many years, precisely because of the strength of the public's affection, clubs treated their captive audience with something very close to contempt. The notion grew up in boardrooms that crowds would always come in the numbers in which they flocked to grounds in the 1950s, and that it was not in the least necessary to improve spectator conditions. During the first sixty years of this century, Glasgow could make a very plausible claim to be regarded as the football capital of the world. For almost all of that period, the city could boast six First Division clubs, two grounds that would and did accommodate more than 100,000 spectators, another that would hold upwards of 80,000, and a fourth with a capacity of 50,000. These hordes would stand on railway sleepers, perilously linked to ash banks, and they would endure the Scottish climate in all its rigorous variety. They provided their own food or feasted upon cold mutton pies of doubtful vintage and pedigree. (A long-standing joke at the ground of Partick Thistle, where for a while the pies were of a brand known as V.C., was that you really should have won it before eating one.) Indifferent tea or Bovril was provided at highly inadequate refreshment huts often located in the least accessible parts of the ground. The toilet facilities would have caused comment even among the less fastidious Indian tribes of the Amazon. Lavatories were noxious and few, as the inhabitants of neighbouring streets knew to their cost.

Where grounds were concerned, Scottish clubs had an obsession with mere size. Glaswegians were proud of the fact that 149,000 spectators had been present at Hampden Park for the match against England in 1937, but not many more than the round 100,000 had actually *seen* the match. The clubs discouraged any active involvement of their supporters in the running of day-to-day affairs, turned their players out in unnumbered strips on the argument that spectators ought to know the team anyway and, before the war, did not issue programmes except for the major matches.

By the time clubs began to think about the need for the provision of better facilities, the big crowds had gone, perhaps for ever. Their return in great numbers is doubtful because the sport has consistently ignored the possibility of attracting women. Even at spectator level, the sport is male-oriented—many men on the terracing of a Saturday afternoon would say bluntly that they are there to escape from their wives and young families. Or, rather, they would have done, for it is just this category of man who, in the last decade, has tended to turn his back upon football. It seems probable that there is a direct link between making women feel unwelcome and out of place, and violence. When one looks at the United States, in many respects a more stressful society than our own, there is an astonishing lack of trouble at major-league baseball matches, which attract comparable crowds. Such crowds are, of course, all seated, but perhaps more significant is their composition, for in the United States baseball-going—and now soccer—is very much a family affair.

Chauvinism and dour destructiveness are the besetting

sins of our football camp-followers. The anti-English sentiment which lies just below the surface of many Scots finds a convenient outlet in the Wembley ritual. When trouble followed the visit of Glasgow Rangers to play Aston Villa in Birmingham—ironically in a friendly match—a Scottish Junior Minister, Mr Harry Ewing, Labour M.P. for Stirling, Falkirk and Grangemouth, appeared on Scottish Television and blamed the affray on Scottish Nationalism. He was castigated for this by an indignant Scottish National Party, but he was right in thinking that nationalism was the cause, perhaps wrong to make the political attribution. There is a dislike for the English as bigger, richer, more influential—never as better. It is a constant grievance that the English refuse to take the international matches as seriously as we do, that they expect a nation of fifty million to dispose of one of five million, and are not prepared to get excited about the prospect. Perhaps fancifully, perhaps not, could there be a regret in the national consciousness for the events of 1707 which led to the Treaty of Union? The hostility of the Lowland Presbyterian Scot towards the Southern Irish may partly have been caused by the suspicion that in choosing the path of resistance, the Irish opted for the nobler course.

So, Highland songs will be sung, tartans will be worn, never mind that many of the gaudily dressed come from family backgrounds with a history of fanatical opposition to the House of Stuart. There has even been some successful pressure over the last five years to replace one dirge, 'God Save the Queen', with another, 'Flower of Scotland', which has the sole saving grace of being *our* dirge.

More damaging to the future of the game in Scotland is the internecine hooliganism, much of it reflecting the racial and religious rivalries of the two kinds of Irishman, the Ulster Scot, and the Nationalist of the other three provinces. From a subject which for half a century was virtually ignored, or its gravity minimised, or the ailment treated with bromides, the reporting of it in the Scottish sporting Press in the last fifteen years has been of an almost universally high calibre. The two clubs themselves were in a genuine dilemma. If they dealt very severely with their offending supporters, there was the possibility that they would permanently alienate their most faithful adherents, even if they were attached to the club for sectarian reasons which had little to do with the purpose for which the club was supposed to exist. If, on the other hand, the clubs did little or nothing, there was the likelihood that the respectable supporter, sickened by the antics of people with whom he would not have associated himself under any other auspices, would desert the game in droves.

No one who observes Scottish football today can seriously doubt that the second of these eventualities took place. Observe the composition of a crowd 'skailing' (to use the Scots word) from a match on a Saturday. The over-sixties are well represented. In their culture, working-men go to a match on a Saturday afternoon. Inevitably, they are a dwindling market. Bands of youths abound—take away the incidents of violence caused by under-twenty-fives, and football would be virtually trouble-free. The people who have largely gone from football are the young family men between twenty-five and forty, the men who traditionally brought along their young sons to watch and so introduced to the game the customers of the next generation.

Clubs have made attempts to deal with crowd trouble, but such attempts have been spasmodic, and there has been resistance to the idea that grounds should be licensed by local authorities in the way that most other places of entertainment are. Some of the club comment on the behaviour of their supporters has been less than frank. At a time when the behaviour of several thousands of Rangers fans both in England and abroad had put the club's continuance in international competition in jeopardy, the club historian, Willie Allison, could write, 'What a pity that the reputation of a great club should be tarnished by the antics of a few madcaps.' It might have been productive if Rangers, Celtic and Hearts, whose supporters have been the principal offenders in recent years, had encouraged the police to lift the offending and offensive songsters from the terracing week after week for a period of several months.

The credit side

The playing down of the less attractive facets of the Scottish football follower's character has in the past rendered a disservice to the game. It would be almost as great a distortion to leave blank the credit side of the ledger. The Scottish fan's generosity is legendary. From the earliest days of professional football, charitable organisations have queued up to be allowed to collect at football matches. For many years local hospitals were heavily indebted to the various Charity Cup competitions, and recently supporters have contributed generously to the provision of commentary facilities for hospitals and for the accommodation of parties of handicapped enthusiasts.

The Scottish fan is wildly unpredictable in his behaviour. There are many occasions on which he will make his compatriots cringe, especially those who are unfortunate enough to be visiting the country to which he is currently paying his attentions. He will, however, behave well on some days on which it would have been logical to expect the worst. Thus, Celtic supporters were in general cheerful and well behaved in Lisbon in 1967, on the occasion of the Scottish side's success in the European Cup Final. The main complaint which the British Embassy had against the Scottish visitors was the inability of many of them to muster the return fare.

It could be argued that in May 1967 victory sweetened tempers, but a more impressive example of self-control came at Wembley in 1975. London Transport employees had refused to carry the Scots fans out to the stadium as a result of several attacks on staff two years before. The Scots were faced with a long walk back to the city centre in the aftermath of a humiliating defeat, England having triumphed by 5-1. When the full-time score was known, people back in Scotland feared the worst, but surprisingly the retreat from Wembley was almost incident-free.

There is, too, in the Scot who watches football every week, a high degree of knowledge and a basic honesty. On two memorable match-days, Scottish crowds behaved superlatively well, perhaps because their natural uncouthness was

Hampden's biggest night, May 1960. Di Stefano puts Real Madrid ahead against Eintracht Frankfurt

ameliorated by the more sophisticated European influence. In May 1960, the European Cup Final was held at Hampden Park, Glasgow. One of the finalists, the German side Eintracht Frankfurt, had thrashed Rangers by 12-4 over two matches in an earlier round. Since the Rangers team of the time was the best in Scotland, not only the Rangers supporters were of the opinion that their conquerors must therefore be the best team in Europe. Certainly all except the Spanish visitors in the 127,000 crowd believed this when the match began. It seemed, when Frankfurt took an early lead, that this was indeed so. Then their opponents, Real Madrid, disclosed that they were the team not only of the year but of the decade, as they proceeded to take Frankfurt apart. By the end of the match, played on an evening which had indeed to be beautiful to complement the standard of play, Real Madrid had scored seven goals in losing three. To the eternal credit of the Scottish public, there was quick and generous recognition of where greatness lay. The prolonged and rapturous reception given to both teams at the end of the game made this the most brilliant and memorable of all European finals to date, and Scotland could share, although vicariously, in a wonderful sporting occasion (see page 71).

The return of the European Cup Final to Glasgow in 1976 saw the Scots again appear to advantage. It is possible that they were impressed by the evident amity which existed between the Frenchmen who had come over with St Etienne and the Germans who were hoping for a Bayern Munich victory. At all events, the fine Scots tradition of hospitality to foreigners was genuinely in evidence, and for a couple of days Glasgow achieved an unfeigned Continental gaiety. No club or national partisanship was called for from the Scots, and they could be objective and simply enjoy the match and bring their knowledge and understanding to bear. In such a situation, where his innate qualities of generosity and humour can find expression, the man swathed in a Lion Rampant, festooned with tartan scarves and tottering beneath an improbable 'bunnet' would be recognised only in appearance by the citizens of Newcastle and points south.

Future Indefinite

IT is certain that the great days of mass attendance at football matches in Scotland have gone. Never again will Rangers play to an aggregate of over one million people in a season, as they did on several occasions in the late 1940s and early '50s. There is no single reason for the drastic reduction in attendance figures over the last twenty years, but several factors have clearly had a major effect.

Perhaps most important, the standard of living in Scotland has risen perceptibly, though much less dramatically than in Europe, or indeed in other areas of the United Kingdom. Football now has to compete with the golf-course, the car, the week-end shopping—since many families now live at some distance from the shops—and even with the garden, in an age when the incidence of home-owning is always increasing

A new and potent rival to Association Football has arisen in the shape of its sister game, Rugby Union. Rugby offers both player and spectator a far superior social life to anything that professional football affords, with infinitely greater opportunities for active involvement in the running of the club both on the playing and the administrative side. To the member, the rugby club is 'my club' in a way that a football club can never be. Even ten years ago it was true to say that rugby flourished only in Edinburgh, in Glasgow to a much lesser degree and in the Borders. Now towns such as Kilmarnock and Inverness, where the game was virtually unknown a mere score of years ago, have thriving sides in the First Division of Scottish League Rugby. Soccer will ignore this new development at its peril.

For all these reasons, gates at soccer matches have declined steeply, and many regular supporters have been driven from the terracing by the repeated mindless acts of violence and obscenity which the clubs initially seemed unwilling to do much about, and latterly have seemed to lack the capability to contain. The hard-pressed clubs were dealt another savage body-blow when, in the aftermath of the Ibrox Disaster of 1971, local authorities set in train plans to restrict severely the number of spectators to be admitted to the larger grounds. Since 1960, to take one example, the capacity of Hampden Park has shrunk from 134,000 to 100,000 to 85,000 and it is unlikely to remain for long even at the last figure quoted.

It would be easy, therefore, to assume that the outlook for the professional game in Scotland is one of unrelieved gloom, that the future will see Scottish football as a very unimportant appendage of the English game. National pride will ensure that this does not happen. Football still sells newspapers, and there is a huge viewing public for the game. It is true that over-dependence on television is undesirable; as long as sponsorship is more important than money taken at the gate, the game is living on a kidney machine. But in the same way that the Englishmen who rarely visit a county ground will bombard the G.P.O. special numbers for Test and County scores, so the Scots will argue vociferously about and make bets on games which they now largely see at second hand.

Certainly, there is no lack of participant enthusiasm in the minor grades. More schoolboys are playing than ever before; often the only limitation on numbers is that imposed by central Scotland's crippling lack of good playing-field facilities. Amateur clubs proliferate, and that peculiarly Scottish grade, Junior football, has not attracted so many spectators since the palmy immediate post-war days.

The fact that Scotland are current British champions has given the game a tremendous fillip, so too the fact that the Scots qualified for the World Cup finals in Argentina—and this although their section included Czechoslovakia, the reigning European champions. The old missionary spirit burns in the blood*—the quality that sent Raith Rovers to

* When the Hapsburgs still ruled the Austro-Hungarian Empire, there was a statue erected in Prague to Johnny Madden, a former Celtic player, who was largely instrumental in introducing the skills of the game to Central Europe.

the Canary Islands (and shipwreck) in the 1920s, the quality that sent Queen of the South, only fractionally less improbably, to Algeria a decade later.

Hampden Park on international match-days remains the nearest thing to a National Assembly that the Scots have. It is an arena wherein spectators and players can exhibit the quality of courage, highly prized by Scots, or allow it to spill over into mindless aggression; it is the place to demonstrate pride of nationality or detestable bad-mannered chauvinism. Above all, it is a pitched field on which Scotland may still defeat the best which the four quarters of the world can send. It is precisely because of this that the Scottish footballer has no credible rival for the position of folk-hero.

A Last Word

THE Scottish Footballer is essentially a creature of that grimly fascinating area which is the industrial central belt. In the century or so that he has been playing, it has been against a background of deprivation which might be alleviated from time to time but could never be banished.

For him, football is a means of releasing pent-up energy, often the only form of artistic expression to which he can aspire, and, for a fortunate few, an escape from the otherwise inevitable subjugation to an industrial society. He has come up in the world during the intervening century. Time was when the acceptance of money for playing was the basis for accusations of moral turpitude. Today, in the spring of 1978, the young man who will wear the dark-blue shirt of Scotland in Argentina is lionised, and few doors are closed against him.

He is the man whom the watchers would like to be, although many of those same watchers may be eminent in eminent callings. He is combative, impatient of discipline, often bearing the seeds of self-destruction. For him, the bravura individual performance will always come more easily than the methodical subordination to a plan devised by others. His gifts are those of the improviser. He is cocky—as well he might be, for he has the chance to become the embodiment of his country, which is given to few of his fellow-countrymen. His solo turns will excite the unstinting admiration of world football opinion and, with his ten colleagues, will give performances such as to make the angels weep. Even today, he will entertain millions without hope of commensurate financial reward. He is, quite simply, the Scottish Footballer.

Reading List

Away Wi' the Goalie! John Fairgrieve (Stanley Paul, 1977).

Celtic, Sir Robert Kelly (Hay Nisbet and Miller, 1971).

The Chester Report, Department of Education and Science, Committee on Football (H.M.S.O., 1968).

English Professional Football, Stephen V. Allera and A. R. Robay (P.E.P., 1966).

The Game for the Game's Sake (Centennial History of Queen's Park F.C.), Robert A. Crampsey (Hay Nisbet, 1967).

'The Labour Market in Professional Football', Peter J. Sloane (*British Journal of Industrial Relations*, Vol. 7, 1969).

On the Spot: Football as a Profession, Derek Dougan (Stanley Paul, 1975).

One Hundred Years of Scottish Football, John Rafferty (Pan Books, 1973).

Rangers: the New Era, William Allison (Rangers F.C., 1966).

The Sash He Never Wore, Derek Dougan (Mayflower, 1974).

We'll Support You Evermore: The Impertinent Saga of Scottish 'Fitba', edited by Ian Archer and Trevor Royle (Souvenir Press, 1976).